GONE, BUT NOT FORGOTTEN

Published in 2004 by

WOODFIELD PUBLISHING
Woodfield House, Babsham Lane, Bognor Regis
West Sussex PO21 5EL, England.

ISBN 1-903953-64-2

Gone, but not Forgotten

A Leicestershire Schoolboy's Recollections of Life During World War Two

STANLEY BLACKMORE

Woodfield

BY THE SAME AUTHOR

CONTENTS

ACKNOWLEDGEMENTS

I am greatly indebted to several of my friends, who have very kindly, and most painstakingly checked the draft manuscript of this book for mistakes in spelling, grammar and punctuation.

Unless credited otherwise, all photographs and illustrations are taken from family albums, and the remaining sketches were made by me at the time of each incident depicted, and are taken from an old notebook.

Stanley Blackmore 2004

1. The Beginning

Nowadays, one would think nothing at all of driving from Leicester to Devon, but in the last year of the 1930s, especially with the uncertain breed of cars we seemed to possess, such journeys were almost bound to be something of an adventure. In the summer of 1939 our family travelled down to Devon for a holiday and when it was over, returned to Leicester in two separate parties. At that time, events in Europe and the possibility of war seemed to be affecting our lives more and more with each day that passed and clearly the news was becoming increasingly serious.

Since his appointment in 1932, for the intervening seven years my father had been Vicar of the large parish of St James the Greater in Leicester, which was towards the outskirts of the city, on the London Road, opposite the wide, open expanse of the Victoria Park. Having been a Chaplain to the Forces in The Great War of 1914-18 he had served in the Diocese of Leicester ever since, having moved to this parish from the living of Rothley, where I had been born in 1929.

My father was clearly worried by events that were taking place and eventually it reached the point when, on 2nd September, he felt that he must immediately return by train, leaving the rest of us to make our own way back on the following day. My mother drove the car, an old Armstrong Siddeley, and my elder brother Courtenay and I were crammed in with all the luggage, complete with the dog.

Sunday 3rd September 1939 started as a lovely sunny day, and we duly set out for home, with no particular misgivings that I can recall, other than to get home safely. There was very little traffic and we were making quite steady progress and enjoying our return journey.

A little before mid-day, however, I can clearly remember us driving through a village on the A-38 south-west of Exeter when we noticed people emerging from the church after Matins and several of the women were crying. My mother suspected what had occurred and stopped to make enquiries. Her worst fears were immediately confirmed when we learnt that war had just been declared with Nazi Germany.

It is hard to remember exactly what emotions this created in us at the time, but I do recall most vividly my mother's anxiety that we should get home safely and as quickly as possible. However, I am afraid that the Fates decreed otherwise, because shortly afterwards, at the top of Haldon Hill near Exeter racecourse, the car came to a grinding halt, having emitted some very unhappy and expensive noises from its nether regions. An extremely helpful garage proprietor came out from Exeter, and quickly diagnosed the failure of the big-end. He towed us to his garage, and promised that he would put the necessary work in hand just as soon as he could obtain the replacement parts. All things considered, however, he admitted that with the outbreak of war it was difficult to say how long it would take.

Obviously there was no alternative other than for us to continue our journey by train, but rumours were rife of the bombing of cities by the Nazi Luftwaffe, and the wholesale evacuation of women and children. My mother spoke to my father on the telephone and it was decided that it would be better to leave me and my brother down in Devon with some cousins who farmed near Hemyock in the Blackdown Hills. Subsequent calls set the wheels in motion and they immediately agreed to this idea; however, my brother was far more forceful, and he refused to allow my mother to continue the journey alone, and eventually persuaded her that I should be left in Devon, and that he should accompany her, the dog, and all of the luggage, back to Leicester.

The rest of the day was spent in making all the necessary arrangements, and it was already dark before enquiries revealed that the last bus from Exeter to Hemyock was shortly due to leave. Without further ado, I was planted on board with my suitcase, and instructions given to the conductor to ensure that I was dropped off safely at the appropriate point. My mother hugged me in a brief and tearful farewell, and I duly set off on what must have been, at the age of ten, the first solo trip of my young life. The journey to Hemyock was just over twenty miles, and due to the fear of imminent air-attack the blinds were pulled down, and as soon as we left Exeter the conductor carefully removed all of the inside light-bulbs, leaving just one lit. To avoid being in any way conspicuous we drove on side-lights, and consequently at a snail's pace. The journey seemed endless and clearly the bus company's time-table went completely by the board.

A mile or so out of Hemyock the driver suddenly spotted a couple of stray sheep in the middle of the road and slammed on his brakes. Fortunately, he managed to avoid hitting them but the abrupt halt sent my suitcase flying off the overhead luggage rack and through the front windscreen, directly beside the driver. It landed in the road, bursting open and depositing my luggage, such as it was, over a surprisingly large area. Everyone got out and was very helpful and my belongings were duly pushed back into the suitcase, the sheep back into the field, and everyone back into the bus; and we continued on our way arriving shortly afterwards at Hemyock, without anything further untoward.

I was met by my 'Uncle' Alec Blackmore, whom I remember as being a large, Dickensian character with an impish smile and a deep, booming voice. We drove back to the farm, which from ancient times had been called 'Palmers'. It was in the valley of the River Culm, on the outskirts of the village of Clayhidon, where our branch of the family had its origins. There I was greeted by his wife 'Aunt' Lucy and their four children, Tom and Dorothy (who were about the same age as my brother Courtenay), Margaret (who was three years older than me) and Marie, who was a year-old baby. They were all very kind to me and immediately made me feel at home, but when the moment arrived that my case was unpacked, a good deal of explanation was necessary regarding the state of my clothes, followed by some much-needed washing.

As things transpired, due to the serious uncertainties which characterized the earliest part of the war, I remained at Palmers for nearly three months, and although I naturally missed my home and family, feeling somewhat apprehensive at the daily news of the war which we heard on the wireless, the sheer joy of living in one of the most beautiful parts of Devon amply made up for this. From the outset, Tom very much took me under his wing, and I can remember many happy times going with him all over the farm during his daily work. Although I cannot have been of much assistance, I helped to bring in the harvest, though due to my lack of skill I unfortunately spiked him with a pitchfork when loading stooks on to a farm wagon, which was quite dreadful, although he was most forgiving. I remember the oft-repeated scene when we stopped for refreshment and the men drank cider from the small wooden kegs which they invariably brought with them. I was always offered some and said how delicious it was, but to be honest I found it extremely rough and I think my facial expression gave me away, because my comment was always greeted with roars of laughter.

Palmers was a lovely old farmhouse with a very happy family atmosphere; its lighting by oil-lamps and candles gave off a nice warm smell which combined with those from the kitchen, where Aunt Lucy showed her prowess as a marvellous cook.

I remember our many happy meals around the table with everyone talking about everything that was going on, in the farm and, of course, in the war. On Sundays, we all went to Clayhidon Church, where Uncle Alec was one of the wardens, and after lunch he would produce a bar of chocolate for each of us, which was typical of his generosity at a time when the obtaining of such things was becoming increasingly difficult, prior to the wartime rationing that was soon to be introduced. There was always plenty of really good food, which was supplemented by the odd rabbit, pigeon or hare which were always available on the farm.

I remember their amusement at my surprise when it came to the first bath night at Palmers, when a tin bath was produced from the wash-house and set down in the middle of the kitchen floor; which, with its black-iron range, was the warmest room in the house. It was filled with kettles of boiling water from the range, and metal jugs of cold water added to achieve just the right temperature. My bath became a fairly public affair with anyone just passing through the kitchen at the time; but I don't suppose that ten-year-olds warranted much privacy in those days. In any case, nobody took the slightest notice.

In the farm workshop I made one or two model battleships from timber off-cuts, and these were launched on the mill-pond above the house; and, although I am sure that I should not have done so, I carved my name on the inside of the granary door. Years after, when I returned to Palmers when I was serving in the Army and on exercise in the area, Alec took me up to the granary to show me my earlier handiwork, which I had completely forgotten, and I was very touched at how much they seemed to value that memento of the first days of the war. During the time that I was at Palmers, my father had gone down to Exeter by train to fetch the car which had been fully repaired, but it was decided that it would be safer to leave me down in Devon.

In the event, there was a long period of 'wait and see' while the opposing forces gathered strength for the forthcoming conflict, and those that had been forecasting that it would all be over by Christmas, were having to think again. All of this was hard to believe in the heart of the Devon countryside, and it was only from the daily news bulletins on the wireless that we realized that something very real and ominous was developing – which was destined to affect all of our lives.

2. The Early Days

Eventually the time came that my father and mother decided that it would be better for me to re-join the family at home. After my thanks and farewells to all at Palmers I was put on a train at Exeter in the safe custody of the guard. In wartime it had become customary for youngsters like myself, who were travelling alone by train, to have a luggage label attached to their lapel and to be duly consigned to the care of the guards on however many trains the journey entailed. One felt rather like an old suitcase being handed over to each of these railway officials, who carefully read the label, but tended to refrain from asking the wearer who they were, where they were going, or even if everything was all right. Perhaps they had learnt from experience that the labels were somewhat more reliable.

At Leicester, my father met me on the platform at the Midland Station; it was marvellous to see him again after such a long time and splendid to be back home. Putting my suitcase into the car, he drove out of the station forecourt and joined the traffic on the London Road. We went up the hill, heading for home, with the familiar sight of trams, cars and people milling around as usual, but with nothing in particular to show since I was last there, that we were now at war with Nazi Germany. Shortly afterwards I saw the front of the church with the vicarage just beyond it. We drove into the well-known gateway and I was safely home again.

I think that I must devote a few words of description to the Church of St James the Greater, which is a highly unusual building, that is to say, unusual within the Church of England. At the time when the building of the church was completed in 1914, just before The Great War, the City of Leicester came within the Diocese of Peterborough and the Bishop at that time, for some reason best known to himself, conceived the idea of building a Basilica based upon the Cathedral of Torcello, close to Venice in northern Italy. It has a long colonnaded nave with side aisles and an apse at its east end. The main facade on the London Road, has two dome-headed towers flanking a high pedimented west end to the nave, which was originally intended to provide the base for a very tall campanile, and I am only glad that it was never built, as in my opinion it would have been completely out of scale and dwarf everything in the vicinity. The church overlooks the grassy tree-lined expanse of the Victoria Park, and certainly provides an arresting sight for those passing-by, and although considered by some to be hideous, it is undoubtedly a fine building of its type.

Immediately alongside, the Vicarage was a pleasant late-Victorian building of two main floors, with several attic rooms above and a basement at the rear, which, due to the sloping site, had direct access into the back garden. This was rectangular in shape, surrounded by walls and fencing, containing one large pear tree which provided some good fruit. There were some loganberries along one wall, a few flowers and roses, and a patch of Golden Rod alongside a gateway on to a footpath which ran right down the side of the church to the rear. This provided a useful short-cut to our local shops on the Mayfield Road and was convenient for my father, giving access to the side door of the church. There was a small patch of garden at the front, where a bit of grass bordered by flower beds containing some shrubs backed by hedging, provided a modicum of privacy and stopped passers-by from actually peering in at the front windows.

After my life in the depths of the countryside I found that things at home had changed quite dramatically. One of my mother's brothers, Uncle Herbert, had come with his family to live with us at the Vicarage, and everything seemed to be happening at a tremendous rate, as day by day we were dealing with endless advice and instructions pertaining to the war.

My arrival home occurred just before Christmas, but on this occasion, instead of putting up decorations, the priority was on such things as blacking-out all the windows and putting strips of sticky paper diagonally across every pane of glass, to prevent fragments flying in all directions in the event of a bomb falling close by. From the declaration of war, food and clothing had been rationed, and petrol very quickly became almost unobtainable. There were so many restrictions that included the use of cinemas, theatres and even churches (at first – but relaxed soon afterwards) to avoid large numbers of people congregating together anywhere that might give rise to extensive casualties in the event of an air-raid. Everything was concentrated upon the 'War Effort', which term encompassed so much and affected almost every facet of our daily lives. It says a great deal for our morale that we did not find ourselves depressed or down-hearted during those dark winter days at the beginning of the war; we were determined not to let it get us down.

As I have already mentioned, we were avid listeners to the Nine O'Clock News, which was broadcast daily on the wireless, and this provided the main source of information regarding affairs at home and abroad in connection with the progress of the war. We learnt that, having failed to secure the peace he thought he had obtained, Prime Minister Neville Chamberlain had resigned and had been replaced by another politician, Winston Churchill. Little did any of us realize at that time what an incredible leader he was to become, providing all of us with the most wonderful example and inspiration that was so vitally important to the country at that critical time.

Every day there would be public announcements, which no doubt contained a good deal of carefully phrased propaganda, exhorting us to: 'tighten our belts ... to establish emergency stores of tinned food but (somewhat paradoxically) not to hoard food ... and to watch out for parachute troops landing!' There were even extraordinary snippets of information regarding the possibility of German spies dressed as nuns, and of course, the risk of Fifth Columnists in our very midst. We were particularly warned not to gossip about things that we might have seen or heard and we were constantly reminded that 'careless talk costs lives' and that 'walls have ears'.

Nowadays, much has been written and shown on television about the escapades of the Home Guard, which was first enrolled as the L.D.V. (Local Defence Volunteers) and made up of any men who were ineligible for call-up in the Armed Forces. There was no hesitation on the part of the public to enrol, and they comprised a large cross-section, including the proverbial butchers and bakers and candlestick makers; most members were old soldiers from The Great War. At first they were not provided with either uniforms or weapons and had to make do with armbands to show who they were and rely upon pitchforks, air-rifles and the odd shotgun. It was several months before they were properly equipped.

Along with all the rest of the clergy, my father had received strict instructions that on no account were the church bells to be rung before services, because these were only to be used to signal an airborne invasion. This regulation continued until, in some part of the country, an over-enthusiastic Home Guard, on seeing a German pilot descending by parachute from his plane that had just been shot down, rang his local church bells. This was heard some distance away by others, who promptly followed suit, and it took some time to sort out the false alarm.

As a direct result, the War Cabinet issued instructions to the effect that church bells should only be rung if more than twenty parachutes were seen descending at any one time. It seemed very strange on Sundays not to hear the customary sound of bell-ringing, and I think it true to say that we missed it very much. In addition to Ration Cards for food, sweets and clothing, it was not very long before everyone was also issued with Identity Cards, which had to be carried around and produced, if asked, to prove who we were. As these did not include photographs, they always struck me as being slightly pointless, as they could very easily have been misused. Another item with which we were all issued was rather more ominous, and that was the Gas Mask which arrived in a small plain cardboard box with a loop of cord attached, to hang round one's neck. In the same box were a couple of small rubber Ear Plugs which could be inserted in one's ears, ostensibly to protect against being deafened by a bomb falling close by. At school, we all had to carry these boxes around everywhere that we went, and placed under our desks in the classrooms, so that they could very quickly be put on, in the event of a gas-attack. This may sound far-fetched, but the Germans had not hesitated to use Mustard Gas in The Great War in the trenches over in France and Belgium, and it seemed all too possible that they might use it again, on a civilian population. The warning for a gas attack was the use of very loud rattles, similar to those used by some fans at football matches, and the repeated blowing of whistles, and I am very relieved to say that we never heard either of these during the whole of the war.

There was also a very real threat of a German aerial invasion using paratroops and gliders, as they had in several of the European countries that they had over-run. Because of this threat, large timber poles were erected in any fields or wide-open spaces, like the Victoria Park opposite the house, which were hopefully intended to deter them from landing.

We began to notice small brick or concrete pill-boxes being erected at strategic positions where they could command the widest field of fire, and concrete blocks were installed at key points to hinder invading tanks or armoured cars. Some of the larger cities had Barrage Balloons flown over the built-up areas, but none were provided for Leicester, as it was not considered a prime target. These were intended to deter low-flying aircraft, and no doubt they proved to be quite effective in some cases, but of course they did nothing to stop bombing from higher altitudes.

Many petrol stations were closed down, as fuel for cars became almost unobtainable for private use, and was strictly rationed for anyone, like my father, who was given an allowance for his work. Even so, he found it increasingly difficult to obtain petrol for the car, and inevitably his visiting of parishioners became less and less. It was not very surprising therefore that a local mechanic was brought in to put it up on blocks of timber, in order to preserve its tyres. Not long after, however, he decided to sell it, as he felt that it would only take one bomb to end its days, and it was better to part with it while it was still sellable. It fetched the sum of just ten pounds, and whether or not the purchaser got a bargain is difficult to say, and as we never saw the car again, I don't know if it even survived the war.

Writing this at the present time, it seems quite astonishing that, from the time of his marriage to my mother, and although very hard-up and only living on his clergy stipend, my father had always been able to afford at least two domestic servants, and that was in no way exceptional for clergymen without private means. At the outbreak of war, we had two maids at the Vicarage, called Doris and Eva, and inevitably we were to lose both of them in quite a short time. In fact, Doris married a man in the RAF called Holman Hunt (not the celebrated artist) and Eva joined the Women's Auxiliary Air Force (WAAF). Their departure from the household came as quite a shock to the system, as my mother had not had occasion to do much cooking previously and consequently she and Aunt Marge (Uncle Herbert's wife) had to take on the task of learning how to feed a large hungry household with very little food except for the basic rations – which were distinctly limited.

Food Rationing had been introduced from the outbreak of war and included many of the most common products, such as meat, sugar, eggs, bacon, butter and margarine. There was very little fruit, and bananas and oranges became completely unobtainable, and we were encouraged to grow our own vegetables. At that time we had no luxuries such as a refrigerator, and deep freezes had not even been thought of. How they managed to keep food fresh, particularly in the summer months, seems quite incredible. Household hints were being broadcast daily over the radio, suggesting how one could devise a meal from almost nothing, including what became known as 'Woolton Pie', which seemed to consist of mostly swedes and potatoes, and had been dreamt-up by the Minister of Food – Lord Woolton, and I only remember it as being particularly unpleasant.

It was inevitable that we soon settled into a weekly routine, whereby one knew in advance exactly what we would be eating at any particular meal; and in an effort to break this pattern, once in a while my mother tried to vary the menu, just to get away from the sheer repetition that seemed so unavoidable. One of her more memorable efforts included a delicious meat pie, which had never featured before in the weekly tariff, and we were all most complimentary, and wondered how on earth she had managed to find the ingredients, because normally the meal on that day would have been sausage rolls. My mother went rather pink, and then admitted that she had merely put the rolls through the mincer, and then given the resulting pie a covering of mashed potato! Whatever the explanation, the effect was marvellous, and the break in routine was worth a lot more.

There was one other occasion that comes to mind, when my mother decided to experiment with a fish pie which seemed rather tasteless, and she found in a cookery-book that a little lemon essence tended to bring out the flavouring. Being generous by nature, we ended up with a rather unusual dish – a lemon pie with a faint fish flavouring ! Not really to be recommended on the whole, unless one happened to be very hungry, but whatever comments were made, I certainly do not recall that anyone left any on their plates. My mother would often refer to the miracle of Feeding the Five Thousand, and I have no doubt that she firmly believed in the philosophy that 'God would provide'. The wonderful thing is, that He undoubtedly did, because time and again we would see a dish of food put on the table, which clearly contained insufficient to feed us all, and yet – by some miracle, there always seemed to be enough. One of her favourite suggestions to anyone helping in the kitchen was, "Spread it over the plate, darling."

Naturally we all lent a hand, trying to help in any way that we could, but this reminds me of one particular example of this that was quite amusing. A frequent addition to our household was Aunt Peggy, who was my Godmother and very Irish. Her husband was serving in the Army, and my father and mother were very happy to have her living with us. She had always been very much one of the family and we were all extremely fond of her, and delighted in her outrageous sense of humour.

The incident occurred when my cousin May also happened to be staying with us, and at the table one day, my father mentioned that he had invited the Bishop of Leicester to come and preach at Matins on the following Sunday; and as he had accepted, it would be very nice if he could stay for lunch afterwards. He emphasized what an honour this was, and that we must all do our very best to make it a special occasion.

My mother embarked upon the necessary preparations, and her only worry was that, having no domestic help, there would be nobody to serve at table for this important guest. However, without telling my father, it was decided that Aunty Peggy and May would dress up in the uniforms that we had kept, and they would act the part as our two maids. As you might imagine, there was a great deal of amusement caused in fitting them out and in rehearsing the parts they were going to play, and we all had the greatest difficulty in getting everything ready, while at the same time keeping it secret from my father.

On the day in question, the Bishop had gone straight to the church, and following the service, my father led him back to the Vicarage. As we had been watching out for them, you can imagine my father's surprise, when on their arrival at the door, it was opened by an immaculately dressed maid, whom he had no difficulty in recognizing. Fortunately he was so astonished that he was literally speechless, and without batting an eyelid, May took the Bishop's hat and coat, and showed him into the Drawing Room, announcing him to my mother and the rest of us as we rose to greet him.

When we went into lunch, the two 'maids' performed impeccably, and their service at table would have done credit to The Ritz. We began to wonder if they might be overdoing it, because they kept inventing reasons for coming into the room and attending to our slightest needs. My father admitted afterwards that at one stage Aunt Peggy made it very difficult for him to keep a straight face, because when she was serving him some vegetables, she whispered to him – asking him not to take too much, and to leave some for them as they were both starving ! Somehow or other, he managed to keep up the pretence, and you can imagine my father and mother's feelings when, on his departure, the Bishop congratulated them on having such marvellous maids.

As the war progressed, we were almost constantly reminded with timely slogans to 'dig for victory' by growing our own fruit and vegetables, and indeed anything to be self-sufficient.

Spurred on by this, Aunt Marge suggested that if we were to dig up the greater part of the lawn, we could grow enough vegetables to help to supplement the food rations for the whole family. Without hesitation my father agreed, and we soon created quite a sizeable vegetable garden, leaving a small area of lawn on which we could sit on sunny days – if we ever had the time to do so.

Another of the wartime government's exhortations was for us all to 'save for victory' and to buy War Bonds, to help in reducing the ever-mounting National Debt – which was paying for the War, and rising into almost countless millions of pounds. However, being a very impecunious family at the best of times, I am afraid that we were unable to contribute little or anything to that particular request. We were also asked to save water, and especially hot water – which meant saving fuel of some sort or another, and the bright suggestion was made that we should 'share a bath with a friend' ! All household scraps had to be carefully separated and used to feed pigs and poultry, and we were asked to save paper and cardboard, and to surrender any unwanted pots and pans. In fact, almost anything that could produce basic materials to assist in the overall War Effort.

We soon noticed that such everyday commodities as lead pencils lost their bright coloured coatings, and remained in unpainted plain wood.

The few books that were published just had plain unprinted cardboard covers, giving a very poor impression. In all these measures, they clearly served a purpose, and it was not long before we became completely accustomed to their appearance. In almost every aspect of our lives, the emphasis was upon economy, saving and cheerfully putting up with all of the inevitable austerity that we were experiencing.

Although at the time, food-rationing seemed very severe, I think there can be little doubt that many people were fitter than at any time in their lives hitherto. The weekly ration of butter and margarine that was allocated for each person seemed very small, and the first task on receiving one's weekly share, was to carefully divide the pats into seven equal portions for each of the next seven days. Encouraged by Aunt Marge, we built a makeshift hen-house at the bottom of the garden, and made a run with high wire netting, introducing half a dozen Rhode Island Red chickens who soon started to lay the most beautiful eggs. Had it not been for them, we would only have had a very few eggs as part of our rations, and we would have been dependent upon the most dreadful austerity item on the 'kitchen front', with the introduction of powdered egg. It was suggested that this should be eaten scrambled on toast, but however skilfully prepared, it still ended up looking like a rather grey-coloured lump of something that was very unappetizing, and bore little resemblance to the real thing. Another product of that time was a tinned-meat called Spam, principally composed of pork, but probably it was better not to ask from which parts of the pig it originated; and in any case, sliced fritters fried in batter were really very good.

Notwithstanding all of this, we seemed to survive the food rationing pretty well, with my mother and aunt taking full credit for their efforts and ingenuity in the kitchen. In fact I can only remember one occasion, when there was nothing suitable with which to make a meal, and so there was no alternative but for us all to troop off to the nearest British Restaurant. These were public eating places set up by The Ministry of Food in the cities, where anyone could obtain a reasonably substantial meal, albeit very plain, but at least it was filling, and considerably better than going hungry. It made me realize, however, that for anyone living in the countryside, food was far less of a problem, as I had discovered when staying at Palmers in the first months of the war.

Earlier on in the war, in order to keep control of the rationing, a rather strange Food Regulation came into force, which concerned the obtaining of food from neutral countries abroad. The rule stated that any 'unsolicited foodstuffs' (a ghastly expression) received through the post, could be retained; but it was strictly forbidden to write to friends or relatives, and ask them to send food. This regulation seemed rather pointless, as one might have thought that any source of extra food would have been welcome. Anyhow, it was perhaps inevitable that the rule was made to be broken, and due to the censorship of all mail, a certain amount of subterfuge and skulduggery was employed in trying to get round it. I can well recall hearing of someone who had written to his cousins in Eire, (which of course was a neutral country), and in his letter he added these words: "I often think of the Dennys of

Limerick, and how I miss them, and how marvellous it would be to see them from time to time…" (For anyone unfamiliar with the firm, it should perhaps be explained that Dennys Limited of Limerick, were very famous manufacturers of pork products). As it turned out, this was a classic example of 'the best laid plans' etc, because the unfortunate sequel to this story, was that our friend received a reply from his cousins, saying: "We can't remember any Dennys – who on earth do you mean?"

One aspect of the food rationing was especially hard on my mother, who had a very sweet tooth. All sweets and chocolate became virtually unobtainable, and the only items available on our Sweet Coupons were very uninteresting things like boiled sweets and barley-sugar which never really tasted like the real thing, as they were invariably sweetened with Saccharine – which was a particularly nasty form of dextrose. Much later on in the progress of the war, my mother received a small parcel from Italy, sent by my brother-in-law, Robert, who was in the King's Own Yorkshire Light Infantry, fighting on the Gothic Line, and she was especially delighted when she found what it contained.

He explained that he had captured some German supplies, which included large bars of plain chocolate, and he had decided to send my mother one of these – knowing how much she would enjoy it. Unfortunately, in transit the parcel somehow got contaminated with lighter fuel, and on arrival smelt very strongly of petrol. Notwithstanding this, we ate up every last bit and enjoyed it thoroughly, even though we had to be careful to avoid anyone smoking nearby.

On the previous page I have referred to the censorship of all our mail and this was something to which we never really became accustomed, because anything sent through the post was liable to be opened and read by the censors and portions either removed (by cutting out) or obliterated (with the use of a heavy blue opaque pencil). This especially applied to all mail to and from abroad as it was clearly of vital importance that nothing should unwittingly be revealed in the contents of a letter which might be of assistance to the enemy. Writing this today, it seems far-fetched, but it was a very real precaution that had to be enforced at that time. The use of the 'blue pencil' became something of a byword and was often used by comedians on the radio to indicate swear-words which were not otherwise allowed to be broadcast. One such comedian, Tommy Trinder, used the catch-phrase "Mind my bike!" To which the usual response was: "You mind your own blue-pencil bike!"

There were a number of Wartime Regulations imposed upon us all, some of which were a bit difficult to understand. For instance, every signpost was removed, along with all indication of place-names that might appear on station platforms, in telephone kiosks, or outside Post Offices, Churches, etc., with the intention of trying to confuse any German paratroops that might land. One cannot help thinking that they would have been provided with maps, and therefore able to find where they were.

This led to some quite amusing incidents, as one might imagine, and I have reason to remember one occasion when we still had the car, and my father took me with him when, for the first time, he went to visit someone who lived some miles outside Leicester and quite a distance away. We set off, and soon after leaving the main road and taking a number of very twisty minor roads, it was not long before we were completely lost. Driving on a bit further, we came upon an elderly farmhand from whom we asked the way. My father was dressed as usual and wearing his clerical collar, but even so, the farmhand looked him up and down very carefully, and after a moment's silence, said that he was not at all sure that he ought to tell us the way, 'as we might be some of them parashooters'. No amount of persuasion on my father's part made the slightest impression, and we drove on for several miles until we found a more helpful response.

Life at the Vicarage continued to be very full, and the only serious mistake that we made, was to give names to the chickens. I cannot remember all of them, but the two plumpest were named Elsie and Doris – after the two Waters sisters that we regularly listened to on the radio. The mistake became apparent when they eventually ceased to lay and were duly consigned to the pot. Although we were hungry, I will never forget our faces when it slipped out that we were about to eat Elsie and Doris; sufficient to say that none of us could eat one particle of the delicious meal, and instead, it was a vegetarian lunch that we consumed that day. Before leaving the subject of home cooking, I am reminded of an unfortunate incident when my father invited a Major Blackmore, whom he had met by chance, and asked him to come for supper. My mother really made an effort to find something nice to give him, and was delighted when she managed to buy a hare which she decided to serve 'jugged'. She was assured that it had already been hung for two days to bring out the flavour, and with a bit of red-currant jelly, should be ideal.

However, when they came to skin it, she and Aunt Marge noticed that it smelt rather high, but put it down to the fact that this often happened when dealing with game. It was duly cooked and served for our evening meal which was a very happy occasion, and Major Blackmore seemed a very pleasant man. The sequel to this little party, however, was very unpleasant – because we all suffered from food-poisoning, and I am afraid that we never clapped eyes on Major Blackmore again, and I only hope we did not kill him! I may say that that was the only occasion during the whole of the war that we ever had that problem, which says a great deal for the wonderful way in which my mother and Aunt Marge managed to feed us all.

Soon after the outbreak of war, my father had been made an Honorary Chaplain to the Forces, and in March 1940, he was appointed as a Canon of Leicester Cathedral. This was clearly a well deserved promotion, and we were all delighted for him. As a small diversion, I think it was he who thought of the idea of us forming our own family 'Wartime Cabinet', and each of us was given an appropriate appointment. My mother became Minister of Home Affairs, and Aunt Marge was naturally best suited to the Minister of Food and Agriculture. My eldest brother Rodney, became Minister of War, and Nancy was appropriately given the Ministry of Health (and Beauty). My brother Courtenay, a confirmed matelot, was inevitably made First Sea Lord, and Uncle Herbert, who could not really decide what he wanted, became Minister Without Portfolio. My father was unanimously chosen as Prime Minister, and I was given a post which I am pretty certain did not exist at Whitehall, which was 'Minister for Blackout Precautions'. This meant that I was responsible for ensuring that the blackout curtains were drawn every night, and re-opened again each morning. Any infringement of this would have invariably resulted in some passing Policeman or Air Raid Warden shouting at the top of their voices 'PUT OUT THAT LIGHT!'

At the outbreak of war I was already at Stoneygate, a small Preparatory School in Leicester. It was about half a mile further out on the London Road and I enjoyed it very much. It was run by a marvellous man called Captain Rudd, who had played cricket for the county and fought with great distinction in The Great War, serving in the Leicestershire Regiment. He had created the school when he left the army, soon after the Armistice, employing the services of a number of other ex-officers to help form the nucleus of his staff. I cannot remember how many boys were at the school, but we were divided into four 'houses' called Minnows, Tadpoles, Seahorses and Sticklebacks, so that a competitive spirit was created, and helped to initiate the concept of esprit-de-corps. (Naturally I thought that Sticklebacks were best, but being one, I may have been somewhat biased.) It is not in the least surprising that Captain Rudd placed great store on the playing of games, and he had a first-rate Games Master called Captain Thomas. It was under his guidance that I actually won the Gym Challenge Cup three years in succession, and had it not been for the war, I would have been allowed to keep it.

Captain Rudd believed in teaching a classical education, and our subjects included Latin and Greek. Outside the back-door of the school, leading to the playground at the rear, there was a covered passageway with a railing alongside, which he called 'The Rubicon', because whenever he felt that some of us boys had misbehaved or gone beyond the point of no return, then that was the moment when we had an appointment with him 'To Cross The Rubicon'. Whenever this occurred, he would lift us bodily up over the railing, bottom uppermost, and give us a good spanking with the flat of his hand, which nearly always reduced everyone to peals of laughter, because it was never done in anger. However we invariably got the message that we had gone a bit too far. At first I started out as a day-boy, as the school was so close to the Vicarage, but after a couple of terms I became a boarder.

It was there that I made my first Crystal Set, and with a pair of earphones, managed to pick up all sorts of radio stations by carefully moving a very fine wire, called the 'cat's whisker', across the surface of the crystal; all of which seemed like sheer magic in those days. Inevitably this got me into a bit of trouble, because one evening I smuggled the set up to the dormitory so that I could listen to the radio in bed after lights out. Hidden under the bedclothes I thought that I would not be detected, as one could hear nothing from it without the use of earphones; but nevertheless, when Captain Rudd was doing his rounds, he must have wondered why I had completely disappeared from view, and pulling back the clothes he caught me red-handed. It was typical that he immediately wanted to put on the earphones himself, just to see how it worked, and only after he had congratulated me on making the set, did he then, almost as an afterthought, ask me to see him next morning at The Rubicon.

As I have already mentioned, it was so close, that I used to walk to and from school along the London Road, and only if it was raining, was I was allowed to go by myself on a tram. At that time, the tramcars in Leicester were a very efficient form of public transport, because at least they could never do anything unexpected, as they were confined to the tramlines on which they ran. These were positioned in the centre of the road, which inevitably meant a good deal of overtaking by other traffic on the near-side, which nowadays seems quite extraordinary, and rather hazardous. In fact it worked very well, because whenever they came to a tram-stop along the route, where passengers could board or alight, the conductor would put out his arm to stop any following traffic. It is interesting to consider that I never recall ever hearing of an accident arising from this manoeuvre, that was taking place hundreds of times a day all over the city. Perhaps drivers were far more tolerant, and of course one has to admit that there was far less traffic in those days.

At the beginning of the war there was a desperate need for raw materials, and any unwanted aluminium pots and pans were especially in demand for the manufacture of aircraft. In addition, the iron railings and gates in front of houses were considered expendable, and I remember the extraordinary sight of workmen with oxy-acetylene burners removing and taking away the railings which surrounded Victoria Park. During The Great War, Captain Rudd had captured, and subsequently retained, a small German howitzer, and this had had pride of place on a stone plinth close to the front entrance of the school. It was typical of him that he immediately offered it for scrap, and we saw it being taken away along with all of the front railings and gates.

One day when I was walking home from school, I noticed something very strange going on. Gangs of workmen were laying long black six-inch diameter iron pipes along the London Road, on the outside of the pavements, with ramps formed in concrete over the pipes at every gateway, so that cars could still have access. The reason for this was that by that time, London had already received the full brunt of the German Blitzkrieg, when it was bombed both day and night by the Luftwaffe. The provincial cities, acting upon the experience learnt in London, were advised to place emergency water-mains on the surface, because bombs could easily damage the normal underground mains, rendering them immediately useless, and difficult to excavate and repair. Clearly, a burst water-main on the surface could be quickly seen, by-passed and eventually restored to full working order. The particular need for a readily accessible water supply was due to the fact that the Luftwaffe made great use of Fire Bomb Raids, when literally hundreds of small incendiary bombs were dropped on to cities, and the fire-brigades were kept fully occupied in trying to prevent the fires from spreading. The sheer volume, however, made most of them impossible to control, and they were often just left to burn themselves out.

Needless to say, this technique employed by the German raiders ensured brilliant illumination of the whole area, making it a simple matter for the second wave of aircraft to identify their targets, before dropping their high-explosive bombs. The common incendiary bombs were about eighteen inches long, and two inches in diameter, fitted with fins at the rear end.

They were dropped in large numbers at a time, but fortunately many of them never ignited. Even so, those that did, could very quickly cause a large fire to develop as they were packed with unpleasant things like phosphorous and magnesium, which quickly generated a great heat, making them difficult to extinguish.

The public were advised to keep buckets of water and sand readily available, so that any un-ignited bombs could be placed in the one, or covered with the contents of the other, and this proved to be fairly effective. What was almost useless, however, was the design of the so-called Stirrup Pumps that were made available to fight any fire which an incendiary bomb might cause. These were intended to be put in a bucket of water, and were fitted with an outside stirrup at the base, in which one placed one's foot, and then frantically pumped up and down on the handle at the top, whilst at the same time directing a small spurt of water out of a rubber hose, attached to the body of the pump. These invariably blocked, due to dirt collecting in the water, or froze solid in the winter, and on the whole were considered far more suitable for watering window boxes.

3. The Developing War in Leicester

At the very beginning of the war, even before general conscription had been brought into effect, four divisions, which were given the name of The British Expeditionary Force (B.E.F.) were sent straight over to France, to assist the French Army against the German invasion.

Between the two World Wars, France had been constructing what was thought to be an invincible line of forts right across their border with Germany, which was called The Maginot Line. Ironically, as things turned out, the German Panzer Divisions merely swept round the ends of the line, or flew their Airborne Divisions straight over it, and I am afraid that it proved to be a complete and very costly failure. It is strange to realize that the Germans also built a corresponding fortified line along their border facing France, which was called The Siegfried Line, and this was equally non-effective, as it was never required, and much criticized by Adolf Hitler when he came into power and established the Nazi movement which was to rule Germany for the next few years.

The whole concept of these two lines of defence was of course based upon the experience of The Great War, when two opposing armies were expected to stand up and face one another, and to battle it out to determine the outcome. Certainly, the Nazi Generals had no intention of fighting any further wars in this way, and instead they created fast moving armoured and mechanized Panzer Divisions; and at the same time concentrated on air-supremacy and the use of air-borne troops, which could be quickly moved to any selected location. Finally, they perfected the idea of whole divisions being dropped by parachute behind the opposing front line, and in this way, they turned the whole concept of attack into a new and terrifyingly efficient war-machine which they called 'Blitzkrieg' (Lightning War).

The French Army, which before the war many had considered to be the largest and finest in the world, just went to pieces, and the Nazi divisions simply swept all before them. The B.E.F. were forced back further and further, until they found themselves with their backs to the sea at a small Channel port called Dunkirk.

Much has been written about the campaign leading up to this situation, and about what Churchill later described as the 'Deliverance of Dunkirk'.

Sufficient to say that in the spate of just nine days, from 27th May to 4th June, 1940, just nine months after the declaration of war, 338,226 British and Allied troops were safely landed back in England from the beaches of Dunkirk. This vast number of men returned with many of them having had to discard their weapons and equipment, and virtually all of their mechanized transport. Having been fighting a rear-guard action non-stop, right up to the moment of their evacuation, many of them were physically and mentally exhausted, and no doubt there were some who must have been very disillusioned and depressed.

The actual evacuation had been carried out by a fleet of about 950 small boats, including fishing smacks and trawlers, ferries, paddle-steamers, life-boats, private yachts and cabin-cruisers – in fact almost anything that could float. Many of these were manned by their civilian owners, who were collected together and placed under the direction of the Royal Navy, and a few destroyers which escorted them over to France. This small armada sailed right in to the shore, and picked up columns of soldiers who had waded out into the sea to get clear of the beaches. They were under constant attack from land and air, and many boats never returned. A sizeable number of French and Belgian troops were also taken off the Dunkirk beaches, but the final rear-guard stand was made by men of the French Army who held off the German advance to the last possible moment, allowing the rest to get safely away. Completely exhausted, and having run out of ammunition, they were virtually powerless to prevent the German advance any longer, and having achieved their near-impossible task they were ordered to surrender, and went into captivity for the remainder of the war.

For all those who got safely away, arrangements were made whereby thousands of these troops were transported by rail from the harbours where they had arrived. They were taken to various towns and cities further inland, to be out of the way of the troops who were left to defend our shores against what seemed to be the imminent danger of a German invasion straight across the Channel. It was a most perilous position to be in, and none of us had any doubts regarding the possible outcome.

I have already mentioned that immediately opposite the Church and Vicarage of St. James the Greater, was the Victoria Park. This was a pretty typical city park, with lines of tall trees along the sides which bordered the roads, and with large wide open areas of grass. Several thousand of the troops from

Dunkirk were brought straight to the park from the railway station, and I can remember the astonishing sight of this vast number of khaki-clad soldiers filling the park as far as the eye could see.

Dunkirk survivors in Victoria Park with the Great War Memorial in background. (photo courtesy of Leicester Mercury)

Fortunately the weather was glorious, and many of them were happy just to lie down and sleep in the sunshine, and to wait eventual re-deployment to army centres and barracks, where they could be re-armed, re-clothed and brought back into fully fighting and operational units.

The impact of their sudden arrival in the park may perhaps be difficult to imagine after all these years, but I am left with the memory of many tired, but still smiling faces, some of them still with minor injuries (the more seriously wounded having been separated on arrival at the various ports, and sent straight to nearby hospitals). To this day, I can remember seeing

Officers and NCOs walking around amongst them, trying to rally together and identify men of their own units who had become separated during the mass exodus.

Naturally, many of them were absolutely filthy, having had no opportunity to wash for days on end, and people from houses bordering the park formed bucket-chains to provide water, so that the men could have the first wash that they had enjoyed for some time. The sight of dozens of them stripping off everything that they wore, and just washing themselves in buckets, standing on the grass in full view of everyone, was something not easily forgotten, and the fact that this caused no surprise nor concern whatsoever. For nearly all of us, it was our first direct contact with the war, and we were spurred on by what has become known as 'The Dunkirk Spirit', which was something that was very tangible.

Although the Army endeavoured to provide food for this vast number, it was totally inadequate, and hundreds of people from the houses in nearby streets brought into the park any food that they could spare, and no doubt in many cases, what they could ill afford to give away.

The soldiers were always reluctant to accept this food, knowing only too well of our own hardships in that respect, but it was pressed upon them by people who would not take 'no' for an answer, and they were extremely grateful. I remember seeing the owner of our small local shop in Mayfield Road handing out tins of fruit and biscuits taken from his shelves, and similar acts were occurring all around us.

The whole experience was one of great excitement at the time, but nevertheless we were all very conscious of the fact that here was part of the Army which had returned from

France, monstrously ill-equipped to continue the fight, and there was a certain desperation in trying to do everything possible to help them, so that they could return to our defence – which was something that seemed all too likely in the immediate future.

My father was kept busy out in the park for most of each day, and often until after dark, circulating amongst the men, and offering what comfort he could by just talking with them; and although he did not smoke them himself, he handed out cigarettes that he had obtained from the local shops. He also invited some of them to come and have a proper hot bath at the Vicarage, at least for as long as the hot water lasted. This was gratefully accepted, and there was a steady coming and going of six at a time, and judging from the splashing and singing that went on, they clearly enjoyed themselves. During one of their quieter spells, when presumably they were more busily engaged in washing, my sister Nancy returned home from work – not knowing about these unusual arrangements – and walked straight into the bathroom, to be confronted by six stark naked soldiers, and I am not really quite sure who was the more confused.

As I have already said, the church stood facing the park, and I remember my father being told by one of the parishioners that there was a large number of soldiers in the church. He immediately left the park, crossing the London Road, and entered the church, where he found some two or three hundred soldiers just sitting or kneeling in the pews, in complete silence. I can recall how moved he was at this sight, and the fact that they had come into the church entirely of their own volition, to give thanks for what many of them must have regarded as a great deliverance – as indeed it was. There and then he sent for the organist, and the two of them conducted a completely impromptu service of thanksgiving, and the singing of such old favourites as 'Onward Christian Soldiers', 'O Valiant Hearts' and similar hymns, had to be heard to be believed, and the sound of their singing brought more and more men across from the park, until the church was almost full to capacity. After the service, many of them asked if they could just stay in the church for a while, to gather their thoughts, and naturally my father agreed.

The troops remained in the Victoria Park for several days, and a great deal of re-organization was taking place during that time, when unit after unit was transferred to some proper camp or barracks to be re-equipped and re-armed. Eventually, the last of them was gone, and there was just the scarred and worn-out turf to provide evidence of their passing. It was a quite extraordinary experience, and the way in which everyone rallied round, and went to their assistance completely un-asked, was one of the most wonderful memories that I will always retain of the Second World War.

There is absolutely no doubt that Hitler intended to follow the Allied evacuation of Dunkirk with the invasion of Britain, but before doing so, he was determined to achieve complete supremacy in the air, so that his fleet of vessels crossing the Channel would be unmolested by the ships of the Royal Navy. From his appointment as head of the Luftwaffe, Field Marshal Hermann Göring, promised Hitler that the Royal Air Force would be decimated in a few weeks. He was proved to be very wrong.

Despite very serious losses, the Hurricanes and Spitfires of the RAF were not only able to hold their own against the Luftwaffe, but the incredible number of bombers that they shot down, resulted in our first, and perhaps most telling, victory of the Second World War. At one time, when the Nazis were concentrating on bombing the fighter airfields, the position became absolutely critical, because our fighters were rapidly running out of suitable places from which they could operate. However, in one of those astonishing twists of fate, (or Hand of God) the whole situation was reversed due entirely to a mistake, which triggered off the most extraordinary sequence of events.

Apparently there had been an unintentional German attack made on London, which, on Churchill's direct orders, was immediately countered by a bombing raid on Berlin, carried out by the RAF.

It seems that Göring had boasted that such a thing could never possibly take place, and that single retaliatory raid caused Adolf Hitler to direct the Luftwaffe to concentrate their bombing raids on London. This was probably his most serious strategic error of the war, because in carrying-out that order, we were given a vital breathing-space in which to repair and renew our fighter airfields. As a result of this, the RAF was able to regain its strength, and in the matter of just a few weeks, they repelled the Luftwaffe attacks on this country. In disgust, Hitler diverted his whole attention to the invasion of Russia, and Britain was saved from an invasion. As was so often the case in the past, the English Channel had been our line of defence, and the action by just a handful of fighter-pilots had saved us all. On the 20th August 1940, addressing The House of

Commons, Winston Churchill summed-up their action in the following unforgettable words: "Never in the field of human conflict, was so much owed by so many to so few."

This action came to be known as The Battle of Britain, and without doubt, it was exactly that. If those fighter-pilots had failed to stop the Luftwaffe offensive, the Germans would have gained supremacy in the air and been able to carry out an invasion, and the whole course of history would have been changed. Living in the Midlands, we never saw any part of this battle, which largely took place off the south and east coasts, but we avidly followed its every moment in the news bulletins broadcast on the wireless. In fact, looking back, I can only remember witnessing the shooting-down of one German aircraft, which occurred over Brighton. My father and I had been spending a few days with one of my mother's brothers, Uncle Kevil, who lived in Burgess Hill, in Sussex. We had gone into Brighton to do some shopping, and happened to see a billboard advertising a wartime film called *Went the Day Well?*, which had been highly praised, and we decided to stay and see it.

The film was being shown at a cinema on the front overlooking the sea, and when we came out afterwards we found a number of people standing around looking up at the sky, where a dog-fight was taking place, several thousand feet above us. It was the first time than I can recall seeing vapour-trails, as the fighters twisted and turned in aerial combat, but they were so high up that we could scarcely hear the sound of the gunfire, nor could we easily make out friend or foe. Suddenly, there was a gasp from the onlookers as we saw one of the planes spiralling down with smoke pouring from its engine, and before it crashed into the sea, just off the front, we clearly saw the German insignia on its fuselage. That was to be my only view of The Battle of Britain.

During those early wartime years, the Vicarage became a centre for servicemen and women posted in the area, and we got to know a great many – some of whom have maintained contact ever since. Quite apart from our own relations, there were a number that we got to know who often introduced us to some of their friends and acquaintances, so that the circle got increasingly wider. Amongst these, we befriended three very nice women who were all senior officers in the Auxiliary Territorial Service (A.T.S. which was the fore-runner of the Women's Royal Army Corps (W.R.A.C.). They came to see us on frequent occasions, and we got to know them very well. Sadly, one of them died quite suddenly, and my father was asked if her funeral could take place at St. James the Greater Church. Naturally he agreed, and it proved to be a very big service attended by a huge congregation, who were mostly servicemen and women of all ranks. In the preparations leading up to this service, the two remaining Senior Commandants – Clare Murcheson and Peggy Horsfall – decided that they would prefer to attend the funeral in mufti (civilian dress). Being next door to the church, they asked my mother if they could possibly change at the Vicarage beforehand, and she was only too willing to do anything that would be of help.

It then transpired that neither of them could find anything suitable in black, and so it turned out that my grandmother offered to lend a couple of her dresses. They were delighted and quick to accept this offer, but they and my mother, Aunt Marge and Aunt Peggy nearly had hysterics, trying to fit them into the dresses, as my grandmother was a very different shape. In order to hold everything together, they had to rely upon several strategically placed safety-pins. Two of my grandmother's wide-brimmed black straw hats were given a covering of black net, and the final result was exactly what was required, even though extremely make-shift.

The occasion was also relieved by another incident, which again reduced them to tears – but ones of laughter. Just before the funeral, Aunt Peggy came into the Drawing Room with a cry of delight, carrying a large box which had just been delivered, which had a label on it which she thought read 'FLOWERS WITH CAKE', and she was saying how kind and thoughtful it was, for someone to have sent a cake for the refreshments after the service. I suppose it gives some sort of indication of the shortage of food that we were all experiencing at the time, but we were reduced to fits of laughter at her bitter disappointment, when it was pointed out to her that the last word on the label was 'CARE'.

Up to this time Leicester had not really experienced an air-raid, although there had been numerous occasions when the sirens had sounded and we had to go to the shelters. A few bombs were sometimes dropped, but in no way could these be described as a concentrated attack. Leicester was the principal centre for the manufacture of boots and shoes, and although there was much diversification of light industry, which was contributing to the War Effort, it was clearly not considered such an important target as other Midland cities, like Derby, with its huge railway works and Rolls Royce; or Coventry and Birmingham, with their numerous armaments and ammunition factories.

Perhaps because of this, the Luftwaffe tended to fly over Leicester before dropping their bombs on those preferred targets, but night after night the sirens would sound soon after dark, and we would then hear the ominous and quite distinctive irregular beat of the German aero engines, as the Junker, Heinkel and Dornier bombers flew across the sky in large formations.

At the time, I did not think very much about it, but in retrospect I greatly value one incident that I experienced soon after the raids on Coventry started. One morning, when we still had the car, my father drove over to attend a meeting in Coventry, and he took me with him for the ride. There was nothing particularly unusual about this, because we all tried to carry on with our normal lives, despite the fact that air-raids were taking place all around us. In fact there had been another raid on Coventry the previous night, and when we got there it was easy to see the clouds of dust in the air, and the smoke rising from buildings that were still ablaze. Directed by the police, my father had to make a number of detours to avoid bomb-damaged streets, but eventually we reached our destination which was a building close to the cathedral. To our horror we found that the cathedral was virtually a smoking ruin, with only the burnt-out shell still standing, alongside the tower and spire which were still intact.

To this day I can see the expression on the faces of the crowds of people who just stood in silence looking at this tragedy. There is a happy sequel to this story, however, because many years later I returned to Coventry in order to see the new cathedral which has been built, and I found it extremely moving to stand inside the roofless shell of the old nave, which now forms an integral part of the new design. It was inevitable that my return visit brought back many memories of that dreadful day, but it also gave me a tremendous sense of achievement, that something so fine as the new cathedral could have risen pheonix-like from the ashes of the old building, which still retained its tower and spire.

Coventry cathedral after the Blitz (photo taken by my late Father).

In the early days of the war, the air-raid shelters which were used varied considerably, and for many, it just meant trying to find almost any safe structure below ground level. Of course, many houses did not possess cellars, and had to rely upon 'Anderson Shelters' (named after Sir John Anderson, the Home Secretary), which were supplied by the government.

These were made of corrugated-iron and measured about six by eight feet, inside. They were buried in one's garden, covered over with the excavated soil, with steps down to the access door at one end. As may be imagined, these were very damp, and often flooded, but I am afraid that it was a case of beggers can't be choosers. Later, a number of brick-built surface shelters were erected in urban areas, which would withstand anything except a direct hit, and in all cases, the essential priority was to provide some sort of protection, wherever needed; and in London, thousands went down into the Underground stations each night, sleeping on the platforms.

We were fortunate in having a cellar beneath the Vicarage, and a number of deck-chairs were kept ready for immediate use, and a pile of blankets and pillows that could be quickly taken down the back stairs from the kitchen. This avoided the necessity of going outside, but there was also an entrance directly on to the back garden, which provided an alternative means of escape if required. We had a basket of games so that we could pass the time playing cards, chess or Monopoly, and a supply of candles, some oil-lamps, and a Valor Oil Stove to provide a bit of much-needed heat when the electricity supply was cut off.

One day we heard an item of news on the wireless, about some unfortunate family that had to swim for their lives, when their cellar flooded due to a burst water-main during an air-raid. My father thought that it would be a good idea to have yet another means of escape, and a neat trapdoor was formed in a corner of the Drawing Room floor, which gave direct access to the cellar.

St. James' Church immediately alongside the Vicarage, was built on a sloping site, with a large Church Room at the rear, at a lower basement level beneath the floor of the church. Many of the local parishioners would come to use this as a shelter during air-raids, and my father had its outside windows completely protected with high walls of sand-bags. The stage at one end was screened-off and used as an A.R.P. (Air Raid Precautions) Post which was manned by a team of local Air-Raid Wardens, which included my father and his curate, The Revd. Oliver Chantler. The wardens wore dark blue boiler-suits and black steel helmets, and it was their task to patrol the local streets, helping people to find shelter, and ensuring that the black-out was being strictly observed, and we were often reminded that even a lighted cigarette could be seen from an aircraft flying at 2,000 feet (which I always tended to doubt), but the authorities adhered to their strict policy of avoiding all naked lights.

Quite apart from bombs of the incendiary and high-explosive variety, the Germans also made use of land mines (which were heavier bombs of tremendous power, fitted with small parachutes), and time-bombs which had delayed-action fuses, so that they would explode several hours after they had landed, intending to cause even greater havoc amongst those clearing up after a raid. There were also a number of defective bombs that failed to explode on impact, but these were equally lethal, because the slightest disturbance was liable to set them off.

One night my father and Oliver Chantler were on duty together out in the streets of the parish. A few bombs had been dropped nearby from an aircraft that must have failed to reach its Coventry target, and had simply off-loaded them as it returned over Leicester. There was a lull in the raid as the bombers had already gone over, but the sky was lit up by the fires from the buildings that had been set ablaze.

It had been a fairly exhausting night, and the two of them decided to take a short rest, and to light their pipes –

considering that it was quite safe to do so, as there was so much light being created from the fires. They found a convenient heap of rubble on which they sat, and lit their pipes, chatting together. Shortly after, a patrolling policeman charged up to them, clearly in a highly excited state, shouting at them to put out their pipes and to run for their lives. They thought this somewhat unreasonable, and they quietly pointed out that the light from their pipes could not possibly be seen by aircraft, due to all the fires; but the policeman explained that the reason for his concern was that they were sitting on an unexploded bomb ! Needless to say they needed no further urging, and all three ran off as fast as their legs could carry them, with the policeman well in the lead.

4. *The Leicester Blitz*

I suppose it was quite inevitable that sooner or later Leicester was to receive the blitzkrieg in earnest and from the 19th to the 21st of November 1940 there were three consecutive nights when the city was subjected to the full onslaught of the Luftwaffe. I can clearly remember seeing German aircraft caught in the beams of searchlights and the anti-aircraft guns firing at the formations overhead, but unfortunately I never saw a plane shot down. Our night-fighters were principally employed over the coast, to try and prevent the bombers coming in over the Channel, or alternatively trying to catch those who had evaded them on their return flight.

From our point of view, it seemed that the Germans were able to carry out their raids almost undisturbed, which was very frustrating, and it felt as though we were virtually undefended.

It was appalling to see the after-effects of the blitz on the mornings after those three nights. Some houses were bombed nearby in Saxby Street and I can remember seeing the results of this a few days later. They were in a terrace of houses and it was just as though three or four of them had never existed; they were literally levelled to the ground. The rooms of the houses on either side were often completely unmarked, still with pictures hanging on the walls, and the glass in the windows unbroken – but, with a completely open side, on what had been the party-wall to the adjoining house.

One bomb fell on the Cricket Pavillion in the Victoria Park, and this produced the strange affect of blowing out all of the windows in the north clerestory of the church. What was so odd was that the glass was all blown outwards – so the minimum amount of clearing-up was needed inside. At the rear of the church, at basement level, the Church Room windows remained completely intact, even though the sandbags protecting one of them had been blown down by the blast.

The burning remains of the Freeman Hardy and Willis boot and shoe factory in
Rutland Street, Leicester after the Blitz.
(photo courtesy of Leicester Mercury)

Some of the overhead power cables for the trams had been brought down close to the Vicarage, and I can remember seeing an engineer, wearing thick rubber gloves, pulling a live cable across the road and sparks flying up into the air when it short-circuited on the steel tramlines. Even so, the tram service was speedily restored to normal.

There was one rather bizarre sequel to the Leicester blitz, because on the morning of the 21st we heard that the Nazi's main propaganda spokesman on the radio had solemnly announced that on the night of the 20th of November the Luftwaffe had successfully set the city of Birmingham on fire. It would seem that they did not know where they were when they bombed Leicester. This spokesman was William Joyce (known as 'Lord Haw-Haw'), an American-born British traitor, who prefaced each broadcast with the words "Chairmanny Calling" – in a very pretentious pseudo upper-class drawl. In 1945 he was brought to trial at The Old Bailey for high treason and duly convicted and executed.

Even though the blitz had produced much loss of life and damage to property, we realized that it was absolutely nothing when compared with what London, Liverpool, Plymouth, Coventry and many other towns had suffered. All over the city, the effects of the bombing could be seen almost everywhere one looked, with houses that had been blasted apart, or totally disintegrated, craters in the roads with broken gas mains ablaze, or water mains gushing forth, with the two elements of fire and water in contention.

On those three nights, I was still at Stoneygate, during one of my weeks there as a boarder. When the sirens started their undulating warning, we gathered up our bed-clothes and pillows, and trooped down to the cellars underneath the school, where wooden bunks had been arranged for us. It was very soon afterwards that we began to hear the eerie whistling sound of bombs falling, and at first these were some distance away, but gradually got closer and closer, with the lights suddenly being extinguished. The whole building was shaking under the impact of some bombs falling close by, and trickles of dust fell from the ceiling above. Candles and oil-lamps were lit, and after we had all been given hot drinks and sandwiches to eat, we were kept occupied by having a sing-song, led by Captain Rudd – who conducted the proceedings, looking very reassuring in his pyjamas and thick woollen dressing-gown. In small groups we were allowed to go to peer out of a narrow slot, beneath the back-door steps of the school, and although we could not see very much, we were very aware that the sky was a bright orange, and it really looked as though the whole city was on fire – as indeed, many parts were. At no time can I recall any of us feeling frightened, it was far more a case of feeling very excited at what was going on.

In the morning after the second night of the blitz, we found that a 50lb bomb had landed smack in the middle of the First XI wicket on the cricket pitch, in the school playing field.

I can remember seeing the groundsman, Frank Bailes, standing with tears running down his cheeks, because wickets like that took many years to perfect, and having been a Leicestershire County Cricketer, he realized only too well what it would take to repair the damage. When he learnt that a former German pupil had joined the Luftwaffe, he was quite convinced that the bomb had been dropped deliberately by him, especially as he had disliked cricket. Personally, I doubt if his bomb-aiming was quite so efficient, even if he did not enjoy playing the game.

From the outbreak of war, we had seen a vast increase in the numbers of people wearing uniform – both men and women.

My eldest brother Rodney, immediately went to enrol in the army, although he was due to sit his Law Finals, despite my parents trying to persuade him to take the exams before doing so. My sister Nancy, also wanted to do something tangible to help, and she enlisted in the Auxiliary Fire Service (A.F.S.) and joined the Leicester City Fire Brigade in an administrative post.

My brother Courtenay was up at Oxford at the beginning of the war, but he had been unable to enlist because he had been crippled with polio from the age of three. When he became President of The Oxford Union, there was one occasion that they had an Admiral Vivian as their guest speaker, and afterwards, Courtenay took the opportunity to tell the admiral that he very much wanted to get into the Royal Navy, but for obvious reasons he was always turned down. He argued that surely he should be able to take some staff job – thus releasing an able-bodied man for active service. The admiral saw his point, and told him to get in touch as soon as he came down from Oxford. He did so, and was immediately given a commission in the Royal Naval Volunteer Reserve (R.N.V.R.), and a position on Admiral Vivian's staff, where he remained for the duration of the war. It was very much the case of everyone wanting to help in whatever way they could, including those who wore no uniform but were in Reserved Occupations due to their specialized skills.

For virtually the whole of next twelve months, the progress of the war seemed doomed to failure of one sort or another. Listening to the news on the wireless each day, we had a fair indication of what was going on, and apart from the weather, the main topic of conversation was the progress of the war. The B.B.C. prefaced each news broadcast by playing four very eerie-sounding notes on a kettledrum, which were the Morse Code letter 'V' (for Victory), and sounded like pom-pom-pom-POM; and every Sunday evening, before the news bulletin, they would play the National Anthems of all the Allied Countries, including those that had been over-run by the Germans. I have no doubt that this must have boosted the morale of those that heard it.

In fact it was not until December 1941 that things became slightly more encouraging with the news that America had declared war, and was now fighting as our principle ally. This was brought about by one single action, made by the Japanese, when without warning they attacked the U.S. Naval Base at Pearl Harbour in the Philippines. During the year of 1942, we seemed to sink down to our very lowest ebb, as almost everything was going against us. By that time, Germany had over-run virtually the whole of Europe, along with Denmark and Norway and most of the countries bordering the Mediterranean, including the Balkans, and they were poised to attack Turkey. If they had done so, they would have gained control of the Dardanelles, stopping any access to the Black Sea, which would have combined with the massive invasion that they had already made of Russia. They had over-run the Crimea and Ukraine, and were dead-set on getting right into Moscow. They had taken most of North Africa, where the German Afrika Corps, under General Rommel, were advancing steadily in an easterly direction towards the absolutely vital targets of Alexandria, Cairo and the Suez Canal, which would have denied us access via the quick route to India, and there is no doubt that their prime objective was the sub-continent.

Bomb-damaged terraced houses in Highfields, Leicester after the Blitz.
(photo courtesy of Leicester Mercury)

The Japanese had already taken Malaya and our Far East base at Singapore, and they were carrying out a massive conquest of the Dutch East Indies, and the Pacific islands which directly threatened Australia and New Zealand. They had invaded Burma, and clearly this was part of their overall strategy to link up with Germany in a two-pronged attack upon India. In fact, The Second World War (W.W.2.) had become quite literally world-wide, far more so than The Great War, which is often referred to as World War One (W.W.1.). Many countries tried to remain neutral, but even they were sometimes brought into the fighting, as for example, when German U-Boats torpedoed neutral merchant ships in mistake for Allied vessels. In fact, Germany's use of submarines had had a very serious affect upon our lifelines from abroad, especially on the Atlantic convoys from America, because sinkings had risen to quite devastating numbers. There had been an appalling loss of life, food, oil, munitions and all of the vitally important materials and equipment that were needed to maintain our livelihood, even perhaps, our continued existence.

For many years, my father had been a subscriber to the National Geographic magazine, and using his copy of their Map of the World, he mounted it on a pin-board, and kept a visual reminder of all that was taking place; using a number of tiny national flags on pins, which he would stick into the map at all the appropriate locations that events were taking place. This revealed all too clearly that towards the end of 1942, things could hardly have looked much worse. Then, at the end of October, 1942, the whole situation suddenly changed for the better. At a small hitherto unknown place called El Alamein in North Africa we not only halted the seemingly un-stoppable advance of the Afrika Corps but actually defeated them and sent them into retreat. There was then a lengthy campaign conducted right across the northern coastline of Africa, with every inch of the way being heavily contested.

With each successive month, the Eighth Army drove back across Egypt, Libya and Tunisia – meeting up with a huge American landing that had taken place in Morocco and

Algeria, which effectively trapped the German and Italian armies, and resulted in their total collapse and surrender. This was followed by the successful Allied invasions of Sicily and Italy, and then the slow progress up through the entire length of Italy, right into the 'Nazi underbelly' – as it was once described. Thousands were taken captive and shipped back to this country, where they were imprisoned in large camps – one of which, at Evington, was not far away, on the outskirts of Leicester. With some of my friends, I cycled out to have a look at them, and for the first time saw our enemies face to face, as they stood looking out from behind the heavily guarded high barbed-wire enclosure.

Some of the more trusty Prisoners of War (POWs) were allowed to leave the camps to work on local farms; they were dressed in plain overalls with large coloured circles sewn on to them, so that there could be no mistaking who and what they were. I can remember hearing that the farmers much preferred the Germans to the Italians, as the latter were inherently lazy, and spent their time singing; whereas the Germans worked hard, and with typical Teutonic thoroughness, did exactly what they were ordered to carry-out.

Thinking back to those enemy prisoners who had been taken in the North African campaign, reminds me of a very strange occurrence, which took place towards the end of December 1942, which concerned one of our own men, who had become a Prisoner of War. One morning my father got up having had a night in which he had been disturbed by an unusual dream, which had been particularly vivid. He told us all about it at breakfast, and acting on my mother's advice, he wrote it down while it was still fresh in his mind.

Apparently, in the dream, and although he had never been there, he had found himself in what he realized was the Western Desert; and there he saw a young soldier beckoning to him. When he went up to him, he found the young man in great distress, and he kept saying to my father "It's me, Padre, Private Appleby, – please tell them." In the dream, my father realized that he did not know the name, nor did he recognize the man by sight, and asked him repeatedly where he came from, and what he could do to help; but as is so often the case in dreams – it was at that point that my father woke up.

However, he felt sufficiently disturbed to investigate the matter further, and first of all, he decided to hunt through the Church Electoral Roll which gave the names of all the parishioners. As his city parish had a population of over two-thousand, it was inevitable that many of them rarely or never came to church, so he felt that it was not altogether surprising that the name meant nothing to him. However, sure enough, in the Roll under the name of Appleby, he found that there was listed a man, his wife, son and daughter, who lived in a street at the far side of the parish, some distance away. There and then he set out to visit them, and finding the house he duly rang the bell. He was admitted by a woman in her fifties who seemed pleased to see him, and was shown into the front parlour.

They got talking, and she told him that her husband was out at work, their daughter was in the A.T.S., and their son was serving in the Army, out in North Africa. She went on to apologise for the fact that none of them ever went to the church, but explained that it was rather a long way, and they had no form of transport of their own, and there were no trams or buses that went anywhere near the church. My father was careful not to mention his dream, and gently enquired how the son was getting on, and if they were managing to get some letters from him.

Obviously the Applebys were very proud of their son, and she was able to tell my father that a few letters had got through and that he was in the best of spirits. She then showed him their son's photograph, and my father had to very carefully control his facial expression when he realized that there was absolutely no doubt that he was the same young soldier who had appeared to him in his dream. Soon after, my father said goodbye, and carried out a bit more visiting on his way home. Apart from the curious fact that he had never known or met Private Appleby or any of his family, he wondered what strange reason could account for his dream; but having discussed it with us, I think that he eventually dismissed it from his mind.

Two or three weeks later, however, he had good reason to think again, because on answering a ring at the front door, my father was confronted by Mrs Appleby and a man whom she introduced as her husband. They came in and it was obvious that they were both very distressed, and my father learnt that they had heard from their son's Commanding Officer, that he had been taken prisoner by the Germans, during the advance on Tripoli. They showed him the letter which they had received, and once again my father had to very carefully suppress his astonishment, when he saw that their son had been captured on the very day that my father had had his dream. Subsequently, he learnt that Private Appleby died in a Prisoner of War Camp in Italy, so he was never able to meet the man who had appeared so vividly to him in that extraordinary experience.

At the end of the Summer Term in 1942 I left Stoneygate School and started as a boarder at Oakham School in Rutland. At that time it was one of the smaller boys public schools and not as well known as its brother school at Uppingham. Rutland was the smallest county in Britain and almost entirely rural in character, having scarcely any industry of any sort.

It was only after I had been at Oakham for about a year that I learnt that my father had been offered and had accepted the living of Bottesford. This was considered by many to be the best in the diocese, and undoubtedly showed how much the Bishop valued my father's service in his years at St James the Greater. In addition, the patron of the living was the Duke of Rutland, whose mother had been particularly fond of my parents for a number of years. With the likelihood of our move into the countryside, my father had got another car, and soon afterwards it was arranged that he and my mother should drive over to Bottesford, and as I happened to be at home on holiday from Oakham, I was able to accompany them on their first visit, to see what was going to be our new home. Naturally I was very excited at the prospect.

I remember that the route that we took from Leicester was by way of Melton Mowbray, and a few miles further on, we branched off on to minor roads which brought us to the edge of an escarpment overlooking a magnificent northerly view, right across The Vale of Belvoir. We were fortunate in having a particularly clear day and we could see for miles and miles; and there, almost in the centre of the Vale, was the high pointed spire of St Mary's Church, Bottesford, which stood out prominently and almost seemed to be beckoning to us. We drove down a steep hill from the top of the escarpment and a few miles further on we came to the village, where we joined a main road. Always heading towards that landmark spire, we took a turning just before the Red Lion Inn and found ourselves in the short length of a wide street with quite an imposing gateway facing us at the far end, which proved to be the entrance of the Rectory. We drove through the open gates, and my father stopped the car. We got out and just stood in silence for a few minutes, trying to take it all in. The rectory was in marked contrast to the Vicarage in Leicester from which we had set out earlier that morning, being a large country house built in about 1700 during the reign of William & Mary.

I don't think one could ever have described it as 'beautiful', but there is absolutely no doubt that it was a fine-looking house, built of stone and red, mellow brick, which gave a very warm, comfortable impression. At first sight it seemed huge, and I can remember my mother looking at all the windows and quietly commenting that somehow or other, we had got to provide rather a lot of blackout curtains.

We were met at the front door by a Major Walford, one of the sons of the former rector, who had died recently, and while my father and mother were shown round the house, I took the opportunity of exploring the grounds, which were vast when compared with the Vicarage garden in Leicester.

My delight may perhaps be imagined, when, on opening a door in a high brick wall, alongside a greenhouse at one side of the garden, I discovered a path providing direct access to the church, with a private footbridge across a small river. On further investigation, this formed a substantial length of the boundary between the Rectory and the churchyard. Later I learnt that it was called the Devon (pronounced 'Deevon'), which was a tributary of the Trent. It was about fifteen feet wide and five deep in the centre of its course, and inclined to be rather muddy, but to me it presented the most wonderful possibilities, and I immediately set my heart on building a boat.

Having looked all round the garden and discovered a coach house and a number of out-buildings and sheds, I eventually went back into the house to re-join my parents, and was immediately struck by the fact that the inside of Bottesford Rectory was so much larger than the Vicarage in Leicester, and of course it had many more rooms – in fact, we were told, thirty-two of them. The worry about black-out was largely removed when we discovered that many of the windows were fitted with shutters.

The Drawing Room had a very fine Adams fireplace and decorative architraves to the doors. Its large windows, with a French door, gave direct access on to a gravel path and the main lawn, which was surrounded by some very fine mature trees including a magnificent Cedar of Lebanon and a huge Copper Beech. The river was largely concealed behind a line of various shrubs and smaller trees, but what immediately caught one's eye, directly opposite the house, was a lovely old packhorse bridge which carried one of the main footpaths to the church from the centre of the village.

Looking back now, with the advantage of hindsight, I can only think that my mother must have been a pretty remarkable person, because even to me as a schoolboy, the house seemed absolutely gigantic, and the thought of actually living in it and occupying all of those seemingly endless rooms was really quite daunting. For her part, however, she seemed to have no worries.

We returned to Leicester feeling very excited at the thought of moving out into the countryside after so many years in the city; but for my father and mother this must have been especially the case, because prior to their time in Leicester, they had nearly always lived in country parishes, and in fact I had been born in Rothley Vicarage in 1929, which had been their previous country living before moving into Leicester in 1932.

The move to Bottesford was made soon afterwards and took place when I was back at school, and my return for the Christmas Holidays was therefore very exciting, as I had so much to discover about our new home. Studying one of my father's Ordnance Survey Maps, I found that the village is located a few miles south of The Three Shires Bush – a coppice marking the intersection of the counties of Leicestershire, Lincolnshire and Nottinghamshire, and is located right in the middle of The Vale of Belvoir.

This lovely valley takes its name from Belvoir Castle, which stands a little way along the same escarpment that we had descended on our first trip to the village. The castle is the seat of the Dukes of Rutland, and is in the very heart of The Shires, which include what many consider to be some of the finest fox-hunting country in the world. There are of course many different hunts, but the Duke of Rutland's Hounds, also known as The Belvoir, is one of the most famous. There are many old sporting prints by such artists as Henry Alken, Cecil Alden, 'Snaffles' and others, which depict this hunt, and quite often they would include the spire of St. Mary's Church Bottesford in the background. As the countryside in the Vale is fairly flat, the spire can be seen for many miles, and is therefore a prominent landmark which is affectionately known in the locality as 'The Lady of The Vale'. It is a beautiful church which has often been described as a small cathedral, and certainly its location, general proportions, its stonework and decorative window tracery could hardly be bettered anywhere in the country.

5. Life at Bottesford Rectory

The Rectory at Bottesford was a most delightful home for us all and we settled in very happily soon after our arrival, despite the fact that the house was lacking in two things which we had taken for granted when living in Leicester. In the first place, there was no mains water supply, and my arms still ache when I remember the number of strokes that were needed to pump up enough water from the well to fill the storage tank in the attic, which took about an hour every day.

The other thing that we missed was having no electricity supply; we had to rely upon candles and paraffin lamps. It was quite a business, as I recall, making certain that there were candles placed in strategic positions, so that we could move around freely without the danger of falling down stairs or tripping over furniture. It seems almost laughable to see these words written today, but it was very much a reality at that time, and one simply had to learn to adjust. The supply of oil in the 'Aladdin' lamps had to be regularly checked and kept topped-up; failure to trim the wicks could result in the most dreadful consequences, because in a very short time a lamp could start to smoke, giving off a fine cloud of sooty particles which could cover everything in the room with a dreadful black, carbon deposit that entailed hours of cleaning-up. You can be sure that, having learnt the hard way, we tried to make certain that this did not happen again.

So far as heating was concerned, every room depended upon its own fireplace, and fortunately there was a plentiful supply of wood, but it meant quite a lot of work in cutting logs and stacking them alongside each fireplace. We also had several 'Valor' paraffin stoves, and Rippingill 'Fyreside Heaters', and these, too, had to be carefully checked in the same way as the oil lamps, and they were inclined to be rather smelly.

In the Morning Room there was an evil-looking coke-burning cast-iron stove which heated the hot-water cylinder in the Bathroom directly above. This often gave off the most dreadful fumes, especially when it had been vigorously riddled to rake out the clinker that regularly formed. I am only amazed that we escaped being poisoned from the fumes, or from carbon-monoxide. The only means of control on that stove was a pretty basic damper, which, if we closed it too much, would put the stove out; or alternatively, if we left it too far open, would cause the water to boil, which produced the most terrifying drumming from the cylinder in the Bathroom above. Whenever this occurred, we had to very carefully run-off some of the hot water into the bath, which spurted out from the tap under tremendous pressure, absolutely scalding hot, making clouds of steam, and the water was coloured bright orange from the rust inside the cylinder.

Perhaps the single most difficult thing about our life in the Rectory was that the winter months could be very cold indeed, particularly when the east wind blew straight across from the nearby Lincolnshire Fens. There were times when we were convinced that it came from even further east, in fact straight from the Urals, and it brought to mind the old saying :

"... When the Wind is in the East,
'Tis neither fit for Man nor Beast ..."

Clearly we could not possibly afford to have fires in every room, and there tended to be some very cold pockets in various parts of the house.

There is little doubt that the main cause of the trouble was the windows, which being of the sash variety, were inclined to be very draughty. One of my principle tasks, therefore, whenever I was at home, was to go round each window of the downstairs rooms that we occupied, putting cotton-wool into the gaps between the sashes and the frames with a blunt knife. This helped a great deal, but even so, I can recall sitting in the Drawing Room in front of a roaring fire, with our fronts almost scorched, while our backs still remained absolutely frozen. It did not take us very long to discover that the best way to keep warm, was to keep busy, and to pile on more woollen clothes.

Even a bed could feel very cold, and at that time rubber hot-water bottles were a rarity, because the rubber was so badly needed for the War Effort. We therefore relied upon very serviceable stone bottles, which were wrapped in a piece of cloth to prevent burning one's feet, and providing a modicum of cushioning for toes, if one happened to forget that the bottle was there. We had a long wooden handled copper bed-warmer, in which some red-hot coals from the Morning Room stove were carefully placed, and it would then be gently moved around inside the bedclothes, which certainly worked quite well, so long as one was careful not to scorch the sheets.

Every winter it snowed, and often it could be several inches deep, and one of our main anxieties was to try and remove it from the large flat branches of the big Cedar of Lebanon in the garden. The weight of snow could cause the branches to bend right down, and there was always the very real risk of them snapping off under the strain. This therefore entailed some fairly hazardous work from the top of a ladder, with a weighted rope, in trying to loop it round individual branches, and then jerking the rope frantically up and down in the hope of shaking the snow off. Apart from the unpleasant result of getting a good deal of snow down one's neck, we were fortunate in never losing a branch while we were there.

After the snow, came the thaw, and sometimes this happened so rapidly that the river could not cope with the increased volume of water, and it quickly flooded. At the point where the river entered the garden, under the packhorse bridge, there was rather a bottle-neck, and there was always the risk of debris blocking the two archways, which had to be watched to prevent damage to the central pier. Quite early on, we had discovered some small lead markers nailed to the stonework, with dates showing the level of high floods in the past; and whenever the water rose, we were concerned to see how the flooding compared with the old levels, because we once estimated that the highest of these that was marked, would have produced about two feet of water on the ground floor of the Rectory, which was not a happy thought. I am very glad to say that our fears were never realized, but we always kept our eyes on it.

During my first Christmas holidays at home from school, I made a sort of box-shaped punt out of an old bier that I found in one of the sheds.

I succeeded in making it fairly waterproof and it floated very well, with only a small amount of water seeping in at some of the seams.

This provided an endless source of entertainment, and I got tremendous pleasure out of poling along the entire length of the river, from the packhorse bridge at one end, down to the road at the other. It was during that same Christmas at Bottesford that I have reason to remember the boat and an amusing incident that occurred. Staying with us on leave was a cousin, George Young, who was a Lieutenant in The 8th King's Royal Irish Hussars. Being over six feet tall, I often wondered how he ever fitted inside one of the tanks with which his regiment was equipped, and I can only presume that he must have stood in the turret, with a lot of him sticking out.

My elder brother Courtenay, who was a Lieutenant in The Royal Naval Volunteer Reserve, was also home on leave, and as customary, both of them were dressed in uniform when they accompanied the rest of us to church on Christmas morning. After the service we returned to the Rectory, crossing the footbridge over the river, when Courtenay suddenly decided to celebrate Christmas by launching my boat. There was snow on the ground, the banks of the river were covered in ice and the water looked extremely cold, black and forbidding. Not surprisingly, this suggestion met with very little enthusiasm, but somehow he managed to persuade George to join him in what – by any standards – seemed a very foolhardy adventure.

The rest of us remained on the bridge, where we had a grand-stand view, and watched the two of them slither down the bank and clamber into the boat, which they managed to pole out into mid-stream. Because the thwarts were covered in ice and snow, they were trying to keep their balance, while they remained standing on the bottom boards. They slowly came downstream towards us, with Courtenay steering, and it was only then that George remarked on the fact that the boat seemed to be leaking – which I have to say was nothing unusual.

My brother, being the nautical part of the duo, issued the order for bailing to commence, but as there was nothing available for this, George had to make the fatal decision to start doing so with his service hat. Very shortly after, something clearly gave way, as the water began to pour into the boat much faster than it could possibly be removed, and it began to sink. Courtenay gave the order to 'abandon ship', shortly followed by 'women and children first'. Those of us standing on the bridge were reduced to hysterical laughter as we watched the water gradually rising round the two of them, with George still frantically bailing, to absolutely no effect and Courtenay standing stiffly to attention and saluting as the water rose up to their chests. It is not in the least surprising that lunch was somewhat delayed that Christmas Day.

As already mentioned, when we were living in Leicester there were times when we were very short of food but that problem was completely resolved upon our arrival in the countryside, where we found that we could always obtain plenty of eggs, milk and fresh vegetables. We also discovered that the Rectory living included several acres of glebe land which were leased to local farmers, but over which the incumbent retained full shooting rights. Using my father's 12-bore shotgun, we could be certain of a regular supply of hares, rabbits, pigeons and the odd partridge, which made the most tremendous difference to our wartime diet.

Thinking of that shotgun reminds me of an incident that occurred during our first summer at Bottesford. In an endeavour to show that he would not allow the war to ruin all our lives, the Duke decided to hold a garden fête up at the castle, in aid of some charity that I don't recall, which was staged in the magnificent setting of a large, tree-lined meadow, immediately below the castle walls.

It was a glorious day and there must have been several hundred people there from all the surrounding villages. There were all sorts of stalls, displays and competitions taking place, and at one point our attention was drawn to the sound of gunfire, which came from one side of the main area, where we found a Clay Pigeon Shooting Competition taking place. Having stood and watched what was going on for a few minutes, somehow or other we managed to persuade my father to enter the competition, although rather against his better judgement. Here I would pause to mention that, having been born and brought-up in Paraguay, he had always owned his own gun and was a first-class shot. On this occasion he was wearing a lightweight, grey summer suit and his usual clerical collar, which, despite his being new to the area, made it obvious that he was one of the local parsons. Most of the other competitors were farmers and when they saw him enter his name there was a good deal of winking and nudging and some quite open laughter – all of which, he completely ignored. Word soon got around that a parson was taking part in the shooting and quite a crowd of onlookers gathered around us. There was mounting excitement, which developed into roars of applause when he went on to win the entire competition. Almost the funniest sequel to the event was to see the expression on the Duke's face when he presented my father with the prize.

Following one of his periodic visits to Leicester, my father returned home with the news that he had been making some enquiries regarding a charity called Queen Anne's Bounty, that was available in certain circumstances for the improvement of clergy property, and he immediately wrote off to see if they would entertain the idea of installing electricity in the Rectory. I have the feeling that he was not too hopeful, and therefore he was absolutely delighted when he received a reply telling him that the work could be put in hand. In a very short time, or so it seemed, estimates were obtained, a price agreed and then came the great day when the electricians actually appeared.

The work was soon completed and from that moment we had the luxury of being able to switch on an electric light wherever we went in the house and oil lamps and candles became things of the past. One of the first items on which my father had insisted was the provision of an electric pump to raise the water up to the tank in the attic, and this proved to be a great success. It was fitted with an automatic switch that activated the pump whenever the level in the tank dropped below a certain point and switched off when it was re-filled.

Looking back, I cannot help thinking that it was somehow typical of both my father and mother that the one never thought of suggesting, nor the other of asking for, any improvements in the kitchen, which remained absolutely archaic by any standards. There were no proper fitments or worktops, and in the scullery, immediately alongside, there was the one and only sink, of the dreadful brown stoneware variety, with large brass taps poised above. Right across the wall beneath the kitchen window there was a huge piece of elm about six inches thick, supported on brick piers at each end, and there was a large built-in dresser with open shelves for the crockery, with cupboards and drawers beneath. The old original cooking range was replaced by a more up-to-date Trianco stove, which was only slightly more efficient – but at least it did not require black-leading.

There was also a very ancient gas stove, served by the village's own supply from a private gas-works, including its own small gasometer, just beside the railway level-crossing on the road leading up to the hamlet of Normanton. So, although the kitchen was reasonably serviceable, there were no frills whatsoever, and certainly no 'mod-cons'. Most of the time we had our meals in the kitchen, for the simple reason that it was a good deal warmer, and in any case it avoided a walk of some twenty paces to the dining room along the stone-flagged passage.

Whenever we had meals there, precautions had to be taken to cover the plates or food dishes with some sort of saucepan lid, if one wanted to avoid the food being stone-cold by the time one sat down at the table.

It is understandable I think, that we tended to congregate in the warmer rooms, and of course the best of these was undoubtedly the bathroom. Inevitably, this could lead to a certain amount of barracking from anyone who wanted to use the room for the purpose for which it was intended, and it was not uncommon to hear someone being requested to 'get a move on' if they were in there for what might seem more than their fair share of time! Immediately alongside the bathroom was the loo – the likes of which had to be seen to be believed. It was long and narrow, with a two-stepped dais at the far end upon which the lavatory stood like a throne. Our predecessors had painted the room in a rather bright blue and from the outset it became known as 'The Blue Lagoon'.

Not very long after we had arrived at the Rectory, an incident occurred which was similar to one that had happened at the Vicarage in Leicester, a few years before. It was sheer coincidence that on both occasions we were sitting in the respective drawing rooms when, without warning, there was an almighty crash, followed by a number of heavy regular thuds. Our first thought was that someone had fallen down the stairs, and we rushed out into the hall to see what had happened. There we found that the chain supporting one of the large family portraits had snapped and that the picture had fallen onto the stairs beneath and cart-wheeled down to the bottom. This did nothing to improve the paintings – of Blackmore and Gardner ancestors – which we were fond of, although they were of no value other than sentiment. They were all oil-paintings on canvas, with heavy decorative gilded frames, and each measured about six feet high by four feet wide.

This second shock to the system prompted my father to have them collected by a very good picture shop in Leicester, called Gatsbys, where they were reduced in size down to something more manageable; I still have four of them to this day.

On our arrival at Bottesford my mother tried to enlist the services of anyone in the village who could lend a hand around the house, but as was the case in Leicester, there were very few women who could manage anything on a regular basis, and we just had to make do with the occasional help. One day however, an old woman in the village, called Miss Winter, came to my mother and told her that she had been looking after an orphan girl who was a bit 'simple'. She wondered if my mother would like to give her a short trial as a domestic help, just to see how she managed. It was pointed out that she would do exactly what she was told, without question, so long as it was clearly explained to her; but she emphasised that one could not hope for, nor rely upon, any sort of intelligence or initiative whatsoever. It was typical of my mother that she immediately agreed, and thereafter we had the services of Miss Ethel Violet Catton, who was known as 'Tettie'. She was a fairly willing learner and quickly became very attached to my mother – whom she insisted upon calling by that name, which used to make me wonder what some people might have thought about this new found 'sister'! She was as strong as an ox – very good at bringing in coal and logs for the fire and doing all of the heavier manual work – which undoubtedly helped my mother.

There was one occasion I would really prefer to forget, but in retrospect it was so funny that I think it must be included. As I have already mentioned, the patron of the living was The Duke of Rutland, who was serving in the Grenadier Guards during the war. When he was home on leave he would often come to church on Sunday mornings, with some of his family or friends who happened to be staying up at the castle. On these occasions, my mother would always invite them to drop in to the Rectory after the service for a glass of sherry, which they frequently accepted ... and that is exactly what took place just after Tetty's arrival.

We were all standing around the fire in the drawing room, chatting together and sipping our sherry, when the door suddenly burst open, and in came Tettie, looking particularly dirty and carrying a bucket of coal in one of those dreadful white-enamelled 'slop pails' (as they were called, conjures up unspeakable thoughts). Without ceremony, she barged her way through to the fire, elbowing aside the Duke, who looked rather startled (as well he might) and proceeded to make up the fire. When my mother gently suggested that the fire was all right and did not really need any more coal, Tetty cheerfully replied as she left the room: "All right mother – but you told me to keep it made up". There was one of those dreadful silences, broken by my mother commenting that it was so difficult to get any help at that time – with which everyone heartily agreed.

One of the things that Tettie particularly enjoyed was feeding the rather motley collection of animals we had amassed, which were ostensibly intended to help eke out our rations. Following the example we had established in Leicester, we obtained some chickens, which were kept in the orchard on the other side of the lane which ran down the side of the Rectory, just opposite my bedroom. They were lorded over by a very strident cockerel who was, perhaps inevitably, named Chanticleer. His crowing each morning could be relied upon to wake the heaviest sleeper, which was sometimes a mixed-blessing, but there was never any fear of over-sleeping. My father, who was educated in the Classical tradition, and remembering his Roman history and the sacred geese of the Capitoline Hill, suggested that we should also have some geese, because they acted as the most effective sentinels and were absolutely guaranteed to warn off any fox or anything else. They could be relied upon to make the most tremendous noise, particularly the gander who, with his steely blue eyes, was especially threatening, unless one happened to be carrying a bucket of food. There was also a fat, solitary and very contented pig called Bertha, that just snuffled around and seemed to get larger day by day. The final member of our small menagerie was a goat called Kidaleativy (after the well-known song at that time). She was intended to produce nourishing milk, but somehow or other we never seemed to get round to that. Unlike most of her kind, she was not unduly smelly, and merely trotted around much more like the pet that she rapidly became. I remember that she had one special trick of jumping up and standing on all four feet on one arm of a deck-chair, which seemed to defy balance and gravity, and we could only presume that there must have been some mountain-goat in her antecedence.

You would have thought that we had learnt our lesson, but I have to admit that once again we made the fatal mistake of naming all of them and allowing many to become pets, and that proved to be our undoing when the time arrived for them to be consigned to the pot. In most cases we simply couldn't face the thought of eating them, with the exception of Bertha, who was professionally dealt with by the local butcher (and certainly not on the premises); the ham, sausages and bacon were extremely good. This cost us nothing, as we had an arrangement with him whereby he took the elderly livestock as payment in kind, which avoided us having to eat them.

In an endeavour to overcome the lack of sugar in our rations, my mother decided to take up beekeeping and, with the help of a local practitioner, a hive was installed along with a swarm of recommended honey-bees. Subsequently, she would often be seen dressed in the most astonishing get-up, with a heavily veiled broad-brimmed hat, attending to their every need.

Following the advice of that apiarian expert, Maurice Maeterlinck, in his book *The Life of the Bee*, she spent hours chatting away to the bees, and singing to them while she gently used a small smoke-producing pair of bellows to waft the odd puff over them, to keep them quiet – especially when it came to the critical moment of removing the honey-combs. I can only presume that they accepted all of this in the spirit in which it was meant, because I cannot recall that she was ever stung. For the rest of us, however, we tended to keep well out of the way during these operations; but we all agreed that the results were splendid, because thereafter we enjoyed our own supply of delicious honey.

For a time, my mother also became addicted to preserving, and we were enlisted to pick fruit and to help with the bottling. I have to admit that this was only partially successful, because in the middle of one night we heard a number of explosions, which we assumed were due to some distant air-raid. The next morning, however, we discovered a great deal of broken glass mixed with quantities of fruit in the store-room, due to the storage jars having exploded due to the process of fermentation – a possibility which I don't think had been fully explained to my mother.

We made mistakes, but at least we were not afraid to try. We also tried bottling eggs in isinglass, but when they eventually appeared on the table they were a rather odd colour and a distinctly peculiar flavour.

However, a number of our attempts at preserving were absolutely splendid, and the various types of jam that we enjoyed provided ample evidence of this. As oranges had become totally unobtainable from the beginning of the war, we could never have marmalade on our toast at breakfast, but we always had our own honey, and some of the less sweet preserves were almost equally enjoyable. Also, we had the great advantage of having our own supply of fruit from the orchard, including apples, pears, damsons and plums.

When we first came to Bottesford in 1943, the village had a population of about 1,000, which included the two nearby hamlets of Easthorpe and Normanton. There were three or four small shops, a Post Office and the Red Lion Inn, which was close to the Rectory. As some of the male members of the family used it quite frequently – it was sometimes also known as 'The Rectory Arms'.

Bottesford was on the branch line from Grantham to Nottingham, and we had our own station, which was accessible by road or by the footpath which crossed the packhorse bridge, and then round the churchyard and across a field. The trains used to run pretty regularly, stopping at every one of the half-dozen or so stations on the line, and because they tended to be on the slow side, we gave them the name of 'Bottesford Flyers'. When I left school immediately after the war and started at the School of Architecture in Nottingham, I was to use those trains daily for seven years. I found the 45-minute journey quite useful for reading up lecture notes or doing the *Daily Telegraph* crossword. If we ever needed to go up to London, the 15-minute train journey in the opposite direction to Grantham was equally useful, because there we joined the main line from King's Cross to Edinburgh, with its frequent express trains.

Living at the Rectory meant that we only had to walk through the churchyard and join the footpath to get to the station, which was very useful, but I do remember on one occasion returning to Bottesford on the last train from Nottingham, where I had stayed to see a particularly violent horror film. As usual, the train arrived at the station at about 11.50 pm and I consequently I found myself walking through the churchyard just as the clock struck midnight. This had often happened in the past and I had not been in the least concerned, but on this occasion I found that I had forgotten my torch, which was inconvenient because it happened to be a very dark night. I was making my way carefully along the path when something very white leapt from the top of a table-tomb just beside me and shot past with a shriek. I covered the last few yards to the bridge and the Rectory gate in record time, and only after I was safely indoors did I consider the fact that it might have been a white cat – but then of course, it might not.

Later in the war, when there was no longer any threat of invasion, the regulation forbidding the ringing of church bells was lifted. Bottesford Church had a particularly fine peal of eight bells and the team of bell-ringers were delighted to be able to resume ringing for services and weekly practices. Competitions were often held when visiting teams came to ring and whenever this occurred one had to expect continuous bell-ringing for hours on end. I seem to recall that one of their special favourites was the ringing of 'Grandsire Triples', which involved 5,040 'changes' (different combinations of eight), which had to be carried-out without any sort of break or interruption and took several hours to complete. Quite apart from the physical concentration placed on the ringers, there was also quite a considerable mental strain placed upon the villagers who lived in close proximity. Although the village was very proud of its bells, I think that there were some who found it all a bit too much.

There is one occasion that comes to mind, when one of these competitions had been going on for most of the day, and I happened to be in one of the small shops in the village. I cannot remember the shop having an actual name-board; it was always referred to by the names of the two women who ran it, Edie and Miss Raynor (I don't think anyone knew Edie's surname). Of the two, Miss Raynor was a very quiet and rather 'genteel' person whereas Edie was distinctly rumbustious, with dark fuzzy hair, large horn-rimmed spectacles and rolled-up sleeves revealing arms of which any blacksmith would have been proud. I was waiting my turn to be served in the shop and we were all complaining about the length of time the din had been going on when a woman in front of me asked for some sliced ham. Edie was sharpening a lethal-looking carving knife on a long steel and asked her how much she would like, but due to the noise of the bells she could not hear the reply, and had to ask for it to be repeated two or three times.

Suddenly, without warning, she stormed out of the shop, marched down the village street towards the church, entered without hesitation and climbed the spiral staircase into the ringing-chamber, where the ringers were deeply concentrating on the extremely complicated change-ringing that was taking place. At the top of her voice she shouted "STOP THAT BLOODY ROW!" The eight visiting ringers and their hosts were absolutely staggered and, needless to say, the whole peal came to a grinding halt and her outburst put a complete stop to the proceedings. Edie returned to the shop, looking rather pleased with herself, and picking up at exactly the point where she had left off, asked the somewhat startled-looking customer "Now then, was it half a pound that you wanted, my dear?"

Our first summer at Bottesford, and indeed every one that followed while we were there, was marked by a fête in aid of the church, held in the Rectory garden, which provided an ideal setting, with the main activities on the large side lawn and teas served on the smaller one at the front. This was really quite a big annual event and involved weeks of preparation. There were all the usual stalls, which certain villagers manned year after year, some of them for longer than anyone could remember, and it was also the occasion each year, when all of the best home-grown floral and vegetable produce was displayed for sale, with all the proceeds going to the church.

There were also a number of different games and competitions, including skittles – where the first prize was traditionally a live piglet, invariably displayed in a small, straw-filled pen alongside the skittle alley. The first prize was usually completely indifferent to what was going on, and just settled down in the straw and dozed off with a seraphic smile on its face. In addition, a keenly-contested darts competition was held each year, for a good looking silver cup. By way of contrast, a local enthusiast laid a length of railway track across one side of the lawn on which a beautiful model steam engine puffed backwards and forwards, carrying about six passengers at a time.

There was also a Beautiful Baby competition to be judged, the result of which could make the judges unpopular with the unsuccessful mothers for the whole of the following year. One event which always caused a lot of amusement was the Beautiful Ankles competition, with the girls hidden behind a screen, just showing their legs below the knee – which was invariably accompanied by much giggling and fairly ribald comments from the male spectators. (I cannot resist adding that my future wife won this two years running).

One year someone produced a model aircraft which swept down across the lawn on an overhead wire and was so designed that by pressing a button at the critical moment a 'bomb' (a dart, actually) could be dropped in the hope of hitting the bullseye on a dartboard laid flat on the ground. However, some of the contestants got a bit too good at doing this and were winning far too much of the prize money, so a 'breakdown' had to be hurriedly arranged.

There were other stalls where ice cream and lemonade (home-made of course) were for sale and a small, brightly coloured tent was erected each year for a fortune-teller called Miss Favell, who dressed up in suitable attire, coming as she did, from a family of gypsies in a nearby village. There was hoop-la and a booth where the blindfolded efforts of contestants to Pin the Tail on the Donkey (not a real one, I hasten to add) caused a great deal of amusement. There was a Bran Tub, Coconut Shy, a Bottle Stall, Tombola and a number of raffles for a range of all sorts of different and quite excellent prizes. Altogether, it was an annual event when most of the people in the village, and its two neighbouring hamlets, all got together and pulled their weight in helping to organize this Fête, and the amount of money that it made for the church was sometimes quite considerable. Of course there was one thing on which we could never rely, and that was the weather, and there were some occasions when, after all that tremendous effort, we would wake up on the morning of the fête, to find the rain pouring down; with no alternative other than to move everything that could be moved into the Village Hall. Naturally when this occurred the church funds were greatly depleted, and one year my father looked into the matter of taking out a 'Pluvious Policy', but the premium for such insurance was far too high to make economic sense. The single most important item on the Fête Committee's agenda each year was to find a suitable person to open it. Naturally, we wanted someone who was well-known and in the public eye, and over the years we had a wonderful selection of different people who performed this task quite admirably. I know only too well how grateful my father was to each and every one of them for getting the Church Fête off to the right start.

As I write this I see that it will shortly be the fifth of November and that immediately reminds me of one Guy Fawkes Night at Bottesford just after the war (during which fireworks had been forbidden – for very obvious reasons). I have already mentioned that some time before he was given the living at Bottesford, my father had received the honour of being made a Canon of the Cathedral, and consequently as customary, he was known as either the Rector or the Canon.

On the night in question, although we had not had any fireworks ourselves, there had been several explosions going off around the village and we had seen several rockets and Roman Candles lighting up the night sky. One particularly loud bang seemed much closer to the house and we went to the front door to investigate – only to see two youngsters running off down the drive. On the doorstep we found the burnt-out case of the firework with the label still clearly legible, and my father was very amused to see that it read: 'The Roaring Cannon'!

Thinking of loud explosions, I am reminded of one Sunday morning during Matins when there was a thunder-storm. The service carried on as usual and nobody took much notice until the moment when the spire was struck by lightning. Fortunately, the whole force of the shock was transmitted straight to earth via the lightning-conductor, but the noise of the strike was devastating and almost indescribable inside the church. There was what seemed to be a long silence, although I suppose it was only a few seconds, before my father, in a perfectly normal voice that betrayed no signs of shock, announced the next Hymn, which happened to be No.51 – 'Lo! He comes with clouds descending'. The singing was a bit shaky at first, but after a few bars we all got back into our stride. However, I could not help noticing that several members of the congregation kept glancing back over their shoulders, looking at the Choir Vestry door at the foot of the tower, as though expecting the imminent arrival of The Almighty Himself.

Like many other self-respecting old houses, Bottesford Rectory had its own ghost, that of Bishop White, one-time Rector of Bottesford, who, after he had become a bishop, got into trouble with his sovereign, the unfortunate King James II, over the question of the Established Church, and along with six other bishops, was committed to The Tower of London.

They were duly tried for sedition but, much to the king's wrath, were found 'not guilty' by the jury and released. Bishop White left a legacy to Bottesford, of which he was apparently very fond, and this consisted of the sum of £10 (a not-inconsiderable amount in those days) which was to be distributed by the incumbent to twenty poor people of the parish, who, each year on the date of his death, could come to the church and there recite The Apostles' Creed, The Lord's

Prayer and The Ten Commandments. Quite a daunting task in these modern times.

My father performed this duty every year, although I think that sometimes he may have been a bit generous when some old parishioner got a bit muddled. As he used to point out, he could not believe that Bishop White would have intended to be absolutely punctilious, and so long as the greater part of his wishes were followed, he would still rest happily in his grave.

Having said that the Rectory was haunted, I think that I should make it perfectly clear that there was no feeling of what is normally attributed to haunted houses. We all felt that Bishop White was a benevolent ghost, and indeed the Rectory had the most marvellous and happy atmosphere about it, and I know that we all regarded it as a wonderful family home. Although it had its snags and practical draw-backs, these could never really detract from its inherent feeling of goodwill. The rooms were all of gracious proportions, and although we had very few good items of antique furniture it was nevertheless very comfortably furnished. I think it true to say that everyone who came to the house, of which there were many, seemed to like it, and clearly enjoyed being there as much as we did. Whenever parish meetings were taking place in the Study, we were perfectly accustomed to seeing numbers of women from the village, who virtually took over the Kitchen while preparing refreshments. My mother never seemed to mind and always made them feel welcome.

I have already mentioned the hamlet of Normanton, which was about 1½ miles north, on the minor road out of the village towards Newark. It only consisted of a few houses scattered along the road, and on the east side were a number of flat fields, which, at the outbreak of war, had been converted into an airfield for the Royal Air Force. It was one of many that were built in a great hurry all over the country, and included the usual collection of hangers and other buildings, which in this case, were mostly grouped at the end of the airfield, furthest away from the hamlet. Its main runway ran almost due north-south, parallel with the road, and ended up aiming directly at the centre of Bottesford, so that every plane taking-off or landing, came straight over the village and had to avoid the tall church spire.

Because of this undoubted hazard, the Air Ministry had arranged for two very bright red warning lights to be rigged up on a cable, and these were kept hoisted at the very top of the spire, alongside the weathercock. We always knew when any flying operations were about to take place, as the lights were only switched on, from the airfield, whenever they were needed. We were told by some of the airmen that we got to know, that the lights could be seen right out over the sea from returning aircraft, and when they saw them, they always knew that they were looking at The Lady of the Vale, and home. I am bound to say the thought often went through our minds, that those same lights might just as easily be seen by German planes. From the glebe land, which was on higher ground, we had a grand-stand view of the airfield, and I frequently used to go and watch the activity taking place, especially when aircraft were landing or taking-off. I could stand in our fields, right at the end of the runway, so that the aircraft were only a few feet above my head, and the noise and vibration was terrific, and I could often see the faces of the pilot and his co-pilot as each plane came over, and sometimes they even found the time to wave to me.

From the outbreak of war, along with many other youngsters of my generation, I had taken a keen interest in Aircraft Identification, and a number of illustrated booklets and charts had been made available to assist in spotting aircraft, and in correctly identifying their type, and whether they were friend or foe.

At the beginning of the war, there were relatively so few different sorts of aircraft, British or German, that the task was not very difficult, but each successive year produced more and more planes, and identification became far more demanding. With the entry of America into the war, this again produced a number of new aircraft, and the whole business of identifying them never ceased to be interesting.

6. The Airfield at Normanton

Only a short time after we came to Bottesford the RAF left Normanton Airfield and were replaced by a detachment of the 9th American Army Airforce. This produced a number of quite interesting side-effects, not least of which was the vast increase in the numbers attending the Saturday night dances (or 'hops' as they were known) in the Village Hall, where the American servicemen were only too delighted to meet the local girls, and no doubt this was fully reciprocated. They always seemed to have sweets and chocolate galore and, of course, the inevitable chewing-gum (the former having become almost unobtainable with the onset of sweet rationing and the latter being completely new to us). They also had a seemingly endless supply of nylons – no doubt intended to pave the way with the local girls. Because of this, there was inevitably a certain amount of envy from our servicemen, in addition to which even the American other-ranks looked as though they were wearing officers' Service Dress, and there was not one of them that did not have one or two rows of medal-ribbons.

This seemed quite extraordinary, because many of the soldiers had only just completed their basic training back in the States. Tactful enquiries revealed that some of these medals were for just that (i.e. training) and there was one other with a mauve ribbon which was called The Purple Heart, which was awarded to any US serviceman who had been injured on active service (but not necessarily in action). Later on we were to meet an American soldier (or 'G.I.', as they were called), who had had a rubbish-bin dropped on his foot when doing fatigues as a raw recruit and had been confined to hospital for a couple of weeks, during which time he was solemnly presented with his Purple Heart.

I suppose it was not very surprising that there were several 'incidents' when they met up with some of our local soldiers and airmen at village dances. Consequently our local police sergeant was kept busy, trying to act the diplomat and endeavouring to keep the peace, but inevitably he had to break up the occasional brawl that took place at the dances. After one particularly large punch-up, the US Commandant at Normanton decided to introduce his own military police to assist in keeping things under control. Thereafter, we had the highly unusual sight of two very large Black American 'Snowdrops' (the equivalent of our Military Police 'Red Caps'), both very smartly turned-out, with their white helmets (hence their nickname), sauntering down the High Street, twirling their two-foot long wooden truncheons. With this show of force things quietened down considerably. It might be worth remembering that at that time most people living in Britain's rural areas had never set eyes on any coloured people – except perhaps in films.

The Christmas following the Americans' arrival comes especially to mind, because my father and mother decided that it might be a nice gesture to invite some of them to share our Christmas Dinner. My father telephoned the Commandant, who was very pleased and said that he would check up to see who might be available. On the morning of Christmas Day, four Americans duly arrived at the Rectory in a Jeep. One was a sergeant member of an aircrew, two of them were ground staff mechanics, but the fourth was an extremely glamorous W.A.A.C. (Women's Army Air Corps) officer, who I remember was called Virginia – after the State from which she came.

We were anxious that they should feel welcome, and they immediately made themselves completely at home, and joined in with the family and other friends to a quite remarkable degree. There were one or two incidents which highlighted the difference in our lifestyles, the first of these occurred when one of them offered my mother a stick of chewing-gum, which she had never even seen before. Not knowing quite what to do, she smiled sweetly and said in the same sort of way, as when a cigarette is offered to a non-smoker: "Thank you very much, but I'm afraid that I don't chew" – which reply, taking place as it did, just before sitting down to a large dinner, produced roars of laughter from all of us.

The second amusing incident took place at the end of the meal when we were still seated at the table, and my mother asked one of the mechanics if he had had enough to eat, and if he would like some more – only to be greeted by the rather unexpected reply "No thanks, Ma'am, I'm stuffed!"

When we sat down around the drawing room fire after dinner, both mechanics stretched out most comfortably on the sofa and then proceeded to remove their boots, and we took this as a quite definite sign that they were really relaxed and enjoying themselves. We played a few of our family games which caused our visitors much hilarity, and sang some carols. Altogether, it was a very happy party and a memorable Christmas Day. The only rather funny sequel, was when my father happened to meet the sergeant in the Post Office a few days later, and asked if they had got safely back to camp. He was told that one of the mechanics had been placed on a charge by Virginia for trying to make a pass at her when they were driving back in the Jeep. As he remarked, it must have been the plum-pudding! A day or so later, the Commandant wrote a particularly nice letter, thanking us all, and saying that one day he would like to reciprocate. For us, that Christmas provided the most marvellous introduction to the Americans, and an example of their total lack of self-consciousness, and the way that they entered into everything, making themselves completely at home.

We got to know a number of other American servicemen at that time, and one in particular, Walter E. Hoffman, Jnr, was a pilot of a Douglas DC3 Dakota; but on occasions he flew a little Auster, (which they seemed to use rather like a Jeep, for running short errands). Once when we were in the garden, one of these flew very low over the house – in fact so low that it had to swerve to avoid the church spire. It circled round several times, coming in across the garden, and on one pass, a small parachute was dropped from the pilot's window. It landed on the lawn, and rushing over to see what it was all about, we found that it had been made from a bit of parachute-silk, about the size of a scarf, with silk cords attached to a 9-inch length of iron pipe, in which was a piece of paper with a brief note from Walter, asking if he could come for supper. As he circled round once again, we waved frantically trying to indicate YES, and he waggled his wings and flew off. We next saw him that evening when he came for the meal, and he had to put up with a ticking-off from my mother, who told him that he really should not fly quite so low. He was suitably abashed and apologetic –

but certainly not for long, as he had an irrepressible sense of humour, and was delighted that he had managed to 'hit the target', as he put it.

In the early months of 1944 we noticed that the airfield up at Normanton had become an absolute hive of industry, with the preparations gradually building up for the Invasion of Europe, which (as we were later to discover) had been given the codename of 'Operation Overlord'. Naturally the actual day and time was kept Top Secret, but at least we all knew that a mammoth sea-borne invasion was planned, involving hundreds of ships of every description. First of all however, complete air-supremacy had to be established, and a vast part of the combined allied air forces was going to be responsible for the protection of the naval armada. There seemed to be a great deal of air activity, with planes flying over almost constantly. In addition and at the same time, a large air-borne force was to be flown across the Channel, to establish bridgeheads inland from the landing beaches, and these were to be dropped by parachute, or flown directly to selected landing sites in gliders.

When I was back at Oakham, we were still kept very aware of this build-up for the invasion, as the American Army Airforce had taken over the nearby airfield at Cottesmore, and we often saw their exercises over the nearby training area, close to the school's sports field on Doncaster Close.

Clearly, as they were our allies, we were anxious to do everything possible to foster good relations, and a number of events were planned by the local people to endeavour to make them feel at home. Amongst these was an idea put up by the captain of the Oakham Town Cricket Club, who had sometimes seen Americans watching them, when they were playing cricket. Whenever he went over to welcome them, they always confessed that they were absolutely baffled by the game and could not begin to understand its rules. He suggested that they might like to make up a side and come and play against the town Eleven, and the Americans were very quick to accept – on the understanding that afterwards, they would challenge the town side to a game of baseball.

The cricket ground at Oakham is in a typically lovely spot which personifies the rural character of Old England, but on the day in question it was to witness the most astonishing sight that its grassy acres had ever seen. Not only did the town side lose the game of baseball (which was perhaps to be expected), but due to the extremely smart American fielding, they were also soundly thrashed in the cricket match! There were a large number of Americans spectators, who, instead of the quiet decorum of a cricket match, shrieked their delight at every hit, and capered about in the most ungainly manner, which was not at all to what we were accustomed. Thereafter, the Americans were keen spectators at every cricket match, and the two games certainly strengthened Anglo-American relations, but we all thought that perhaps the Town Eleven got more than they had bargained for.

As in most parts of the country, the Americans' arrival had visibly changed the whole character of the areas in which they were based, and this was certainly true of Rutland, which had been distinctly rural, and had never before seen anything quite like it, with their sheer force of numbers in planes, vehicles and servicemen. Similarly as at Bottesford, the unit based at Cottesmore also had Dakotas, and we frequently saw them flying over in formations that often seemed closer than one might have thought necessary. But we were told that this had to be done, to ensure that when dropping over a selected site, the paratroops would all be closely bunched together, and able to re-form much more speedily on landing. On two separate occasions we were to be forcibly reminded of the inherent dangers which were perhaps inevitable in such operations. One afternoon when we were playing cricket, we looked up to watch dozens of men jumping out of the aircraft and descending on the nearby training area, as we had often seen before. On this occasion however, one of the parachutes failed to open, and we clearly witnessed the appalling sight of a soldier plummeting to his death.

A series of red Very-light signals put an immediate stop to the exercises, but they were resumed the next day as though nothing had happened. The other incident was far worse, because we saw the even more terrible sight of the wing-tips of two aircraft touching, while flying in another close formation of Dakotas, and the instantaneous explosion as the fuel tanks of the two planes ignited, and still entangled together, they crashed to the ground in a flaming mass, with all of the paratroops still on board. On each occasion, nobody could fail to have been appalled, but there was absolutely nothing that we could do to help in any way, and after a shocked pause and possibly a few private prayers, the cricket match was resumed. That may sound callous, but we had become accustomed to such things, with the dreadful affects of bombing, in which some boys' parents had been killed, and we all had to accept the fact that this was just another, albeit dreadful, facet of the times we were living in.

A number of old boys from the school had already been killed in action; they had been with us only a few months before and it seemed incredible that they should have died so soon after joining-up, and perhaps because of this, the impact of their deaths was made more poignant. And yet we all knew that we just had to carry on as though nothing had happened, and try to forget – but the very fact that I am writing this 58 years later proves that we could never do so, and I am not in the least ashamed of the fact.

Like most boys' public schools at that time, Oakham had its own contingent of the O.T.C. (Officers' Training Corps), which was under the command of an ex-regular officer, who happened to be the Science Master. He had managed to obtain some quite modern equipment, which was remarkable when you consider that we were in the middle of a war, when the emphasis was on the three services rather than schoolboys.

We had some old Martini-action rifles dating from The Great War, but he had also somehow managed to acquire a number of Short Lee-Enfield .303 rifles and bayonets which were currently in use, along with some Sten Light Machine Guns of 0.38 calibre and a few 0.45 revolvers. In addition, he had somehow got hold of two types of wireless set, known as the Type 18 and 38, with which we were able to carry out quite sophisticated wireless training. We were very keen to try to be as professional as possible and spent a good deal of time in foot and rifle drill. We were never allowed to fire any of the weapons with the ammunition for which they were designed, but we did spend quite a lot of time on the indoor range with 0.22 calibre rifles and I was delighted to earn the coveted First

Class Shot badge, which was duly sewn on to the sleeve of my battle-dress blouse.

There was quite a pleasure getting into proper military uniform and feeling as though we were actually part of the armed services, although of course we were not. We had our own Corps of Drums, which included Side and Tenor Drums, Bass Drum and Cymbals, Fifes and Bugles. I opted to play a fife, and hours were spent in practicing, when all novices were consigned to the most distant parts of the school premises, in view of the often excruciating sounds that emerged, but eventually we became quite proficient, and the Drums were actually invited to lead parades in the town, and to Beat Retreat on the playing field at the end of Speech Days when parents were present.

Every so often the entire contingent would be taken out in buses to the nearby countryside for Field Days, when we would go through section and platoon exercises in attack and defence. Once a year there was a General Inspection made by some visiting senior officer (usually a Brigadier or Major-General), and we would spend hours preparing for this very special parade, and blanco-ing belts and gaiters and polishing boots and our musical instruments.

Our uniforms were exactly similar to those of the regular army, and we had our own shoulder flashes and cap badge, which was based upon the Bengal Tiger used by The Leicestershire Regiment (Rutland having no county regiment of its own). At one point during my time in the O.T.C. we were all absolutely incensed when we were told that we could no longer use that name for the contingent, and that we were to be known as the J.T.C. (Junior Training Corps), and the reason given for this change was that the War Department did not want us to be confused with the regular army's OCTUs (Officer Training Corps Units). As a sop to our injured pride we were all given small button-hole badges which we were allowed to wear in the lapels of our school uniform jackets, but I am afraid that it did not feel the same to be reduced to a 'Junior' designation.

I remember that our Drum Major spent hours marching up and down swinging and twirling the practice mace, which was exactly the same weight as the one used for all ceremonial occasions. This was beautifully made with a Bengal Tiger on its decorative top, and inevitably very prone to damage if dropped, and he was very conscious of the disgrace that would be incurred if he was to accidentally let it fall on parade, but fortunately I do not recall that this ever happened. We all took tremendous pride in our turn-out for the Corps parades, and anyone who let the side down was subject to a good deal of criticism. Looking back, I realize that we were only playing at being soldiers, but it meant a lot to us and felt very real at the time, and it prepared us for the moment that we would be called-up to serve in the armed forces.

With the thousands of American servicemen and other soldiers from abroad, and the huge influx of refugee immigrants from the European countries that had been over-run by the Germans, there was a marked increase in the population, and finding sufficient food to satisfy the demand was a real dilemma.

To our delight, one day at Oakham, we were told that instead of lessons, we would be going out to some of the local farms for the day, taking packed lunches with us, so that we could help to bring in the potato harvest. We went in one of the local buses out to a nearby farm, where we were met by the owner, who looked somewhat dubious (as well he might). He led the way up a muddy track to a vast field of potatoes which had an extremely dilapidated Fordson tractor, pulling some sort of harrow that up-rooted the crop, leaving the potatoes lying on the surface ready for picking. Looking at the size of the field, we instantly became somewhat less enthusiastic, but we cheered up when we saw that we would be working alongside some Land Girls. These were another by-product of the War, who spent their time working for a minimal wage on farms all over the country. Clad in their green jumpers and brown corduroy breeches, they could look quite attractive, but on this occasion we seemed to have been landed with some that were distinctly 'broad in the beam' and inclined to regard us boys as less than useful. I have to admit that they were probably right, because after about half an hour, most of us had had enough of the back-breaking work.

Returning home for the Easter holidays, I found that there was a frenzy of activity up at the airfield, and learnt that it had been one of those chosen for part of the force of airborne troops. Cycling up to watch what was going on, I witnessed something quite new that was taking place due to the introduction of troop-carrying gliders, which were towed behind the Dakotas. There was concentrated training going on, to see how quickly the troops could be landed, as the gliders and the aircraft pulling them were extremely vulnerable to attack by German fighters. Because of this, the technique adopted for landing these gliders was somewhat hair-raising, even seen from the safety of the ground, and must have been traumatic, to say the least, for the soldiers being carried inside them. Formations of Dakotas, towing one or two gliders, would come across the airfield at about 3,000 feet and then suddenly, on some pre-arranged signal, the tow-ropes would be released from the nose of each glider, and the towing aircraft would immediately climb up out of their way. From that moment, it was up to each individual glider-pilot to select the shortest and safest route to the ground, whilst at the same time avoiding all the other gliders, which seemed to fill the air.

It speaks volumes for their skill, because I never saw two collide in this mid-air mêlée, and the way in which they achieved a rapid descent, was quite simply by putting the gliders into what looked like an almost vertical nose-dive, and just hurtling towards the ground. I can still hear the sound of the wind rushing past the wings and fuselages of the gliders as they plummeted to earth, and at what must have been only about fifty feet above the ground, they would suddenly be pulled up sharply out of the dive, and then in a very short distance, settle down to the ground where they skidded to a halt.

The gliders were not fitted with any form of wheeled under-carriage, but had two small runners fixed beneath the fuselage, rather like a sledge, which meant of course that they hoped to land on something reasonably flat, and preferably soft. On more than one occasion I saw a glider caught up on some snag in the ground surface, and turn completely over on its nose ending upside-down, and I can well imagine the language of the occupants when this occurred.

A few weeks later, having watched these small American Waco troop-carrying gliders, I was astonished to see the appearance of two much larger types of glider, which were introduced in order to carry increased numbers of troops and even light mechanized weapons and Jeeps.

They went under the splendid names of early British chieftains, namely Horsa and Hamilcar, and appeared to be nearly as big as the Dakotas and almost too large to be towed up from the ground. It was then, for the first time, that we saw much larger four-engined aircraft being employed for towing – bombers like the Halifax, Lancaster and Albemarle.

As some of the airfields did not have long enough runways to accommodate aircraft of this size they developed the idea of plucking the gliders off the ground, by rigging up the end of their tow-ropes on high frames, and then catching these on a hook device lowered beneath the tow-planes, as they flew low over the ground – a technique which they called 'The Snatch'. It is difficult to imagine what the sudden jerk must have been like for those that were packed inside, and I always wondered how on earth the gliders were strong enough to withstand the appalling strain of that first pull up from a stationary position on the ground, to flying behind a tow-plane moving at not less than 200 mph. Also, I could not help thinking of the result, if the glider proved too heavy to pluck off the ground – dragging the towing aircraft into an appalling smash, which was a simply ghastly thought. Once in the air, these large gliders seemed to fly with the greatest of ease, and from the moment they were released from the towing aircraft, they instantly became a completely free entity, capable of soaring and wheeling across the sky. I can remember reading in Churchill's *History of The Second World War*, that there was quite a difficulty at the time in finding suitable aircraft capable of lifting these heavier gliders, and in retrospect he mentioned that the military historians were agreed that the whole concept of using glider-borne troops certainly served their purpose, but nevertheless they were a very costly venture when one considers that they were only designed and intended for a one-way, non-return trip. After D-Day, I remember seeing photographs of some of the Landing Zones strewn with broken gliders, and yet I understand that the number of casualties occurring in them was relatively small – but of course it all depends what one means by 'relatively'.

Thinking back to those photographs, I also recall seeing absolutely hair-raising newsreel pictures, taken by a cameraman actually sitting beside one of the glider-pilots when going in to land at Arnhem, which showed that near-vertical dive that I have already described. What it must have been like for the troops, squashed into the very cramped conditions with all of their weapons and equipment, is almost unthinkable – but that is exactly what they did; and in doing so achieved precisely what was intended, with large numbers of soldiers positioned deep behind enemy lines. When I think back to the Battle of Arnhem (which was given the codename 'Market Garden') I am reminded that its lack of success was not due to any failure on the part of the Airborne troops. On the contrary, they gained great prestige from their stand against vastly superior numbers. The reason for the dreadful loss of life was due to some mis-assessments in the planning of the operation, and the much stronger German forces that were found to be in the area than had been realized, coupled with the consequent delay in producing the necessary and vitally important back-up.

Of course nowadays we have the pictorial information provided by television, but during the war we only had the newspapers and the few magazines that were published, neither of which contained many photographs. After the ban on congregating in public places was lifted, we occasionally went to the local picture house (as it was called), where we could see films, which were mostly based upon the war, and always included newsreels that showed what was going on.

We had The British Movietone News, which was very British 'stiff upper lip', and full of stirring escapades being undertaken by "our brave lads in the Navy, the Army and the Air Force" who were "teaching those Nazi thugs a lesson they would never forget." In addition, an American newsreel called 'The March of Time' was cram full of propaganda but very well done, and provided us at home with our only visible record of what was taking place. Inevitably, we tend to think that photography is now at its peak, and certainly there is a very high standard which can be seen from day to day in all forms of the media. However, there was an incredibly high level of photographic reporting carried out during the war, and many news-cameramen went right into the worst of the action in order to get close-up photographs of the fighting that was taking place at the time. As soon as it was first produced, my father took out a subscription for *The Pictorial History of The Second World War* published by Hutchinsons, and I can remember avidly reading and studying each monthly issue. It was only to be expected that some of the war correspondents and newsreel cameramen were killed in action, right up beside the troops who were fighting, and the many films and publications which they produced provide ample testimony of their dedication, courage and expertise.

We were all very conscious that there was a substantial increase in tension as we moved into the Summer of 1944, and we knew that the Second Front was going to occur almost any day, but for obvious reasons we did not know when this would actually take place.

The morning of 6th June was just like many other summer mornings, and it was only when we heard the news on the wireless at breakfast that we realized that it was the long-awaited D-Day, and that allied forces had landed in strength, in Normandy and in the Cherbourg Peninsula.

From that moment, seemingly endless formations of aircraft flew overhead, with a massive take-off from Normanton, of towing aircraft and gliders. Hitherto, all aircraft had been painted in camouflage colouring, but on D-Day we saw that in addition, they had all been given three large white lines painted across each wing, and over the centre of the body just in front of the tailplane. This was, of course, a quick and effective means of identification for all allied aircraft on that fateful day and those that immediately followed.

Clearly, the gliders were not coming back to Normanton, where the whole pattern changed after D-Day, with its Dakotas employed as air-ambulances, bringing back the injured, who were then transported to various hospitals in the area. Day and night we had a constant flow of planes coming in and going out, which emphasised the fact that from that moment on, our entire thought and effort was devoted to maintaining a concentrated build-up of the massive armed force and all its attendant support. There was a steady flow of men, materials and munitions across the Channel, to increase the strength of the invasion force, very rapidly leading up to the break-out from the Normandy beach-head.

As the offensive developed, and matters that had been kept secret became known to us all, we learnt of some quite astonishing items that had been prepared for the Normandy landings. Without doubt, the construction of two floating 'Mulberry' harbours was one of the most amazing engineering feats of the war. These harbours weighing 1½ million tons in total were comprised of 400 sections, built all around the UK. The sections were then towed to the south coast, where they were submerged, to avoid being spotted by German air reconnaissance. Immediately following the initial assault landings, they were towed across the Channel and assembled at St Laurent and Arromanches, an operation which involved 10,000 engineers and 132 tugs.

Making use of these two man-made harbours, deep water vessels were able to moor far out from the beaches, and safely unload the constant stream of men and equipment that was needed for the follow-up to the initial beach-head offensive. Long after the war, when the details were no longer secret, it was revealed that the concept of these floating, man-made harbours was entirely due to Winston Churchill, who realized that sufficient quantities of men and materials could never be put ashore directly onto the beaches and that the Channel ports were all too heavily defended and could not be relied upon to provide docking and off-loading facilities. The actual designs and details of the two harbours were entrusted to some Royal Engineer officers who were virtually given carte-blanche, and a vast labour force was placed at their disposal to carry out this mammoth undertaking.

When it became known that the idea was to have floating harbours, the Royal Navy immediately stepped in and declared that anything afloat came within their jurisdiction, but the R.E. won the day, with the Prime Minister's backing, and the two Mulberries remained an Army responsibility from start to finish.

Although one might be excused for thinking to the contrary, from the films and books that have been produced since the war, the initial D-Day invasion was NOT just an American achievement – in fact there were only 57,500 US troops, compared with 75,215 British and Canadian soldiers. The actual landings were made on five principal beaches, code-named Utah, Omaha, Gold, Juno and Sword. The first two of these were used by the US 1st Army and the other three by the British 2nd Army which included three units of Royal Marine Commandos and a large number of Canadian forces. In the first six days after the landings, no less than 326,000 men crossed the Channel, along with 54,000 vehicles and 104,000 tons of supplies – altogether an astonishing undertaking.

To get some idea of the follow-up that was required, one only has to consider that by 30th June, in the span of just three weeks, those numbers had risen to 850,279 men, 148,803 vehicles and 570,505 tons of supplies which had been safely landed in Normandy.

A great deal of this was made possible due to the two Mulberry harbours, with the Americans using the one positioned at St Laurent and the British and Canadians using the other at Arromanches. Shortly after they were installed, the

R.E. Brigadier who was principally responsible for their design, was warned of impending bad weather by the weather forecasters and issued instructions that additional anchors should be attached to every pontoon, which supported the floating roadways linking the harbours to the shore. This was duly carried out on the British Mulberry, but regrettably the Americans did not think fit to comply with this warning, and on 19th June the Mulberry at St Laurent was effectively destroyed by a heavy storm, making it no longer operable. Fortunately, by that time the main impetus had already been achieved and the British Mulberry at Arromanches continued to be fully operational up to December 1944, by which time it was no longer required.

Another vital factor in the success of the landings was the problem of delivering sufficient quantities of fuel that would be needed for the mass of tanks and armoured vehicles involved in the invasion force. This was achieved during the assault phase, by pumping fuel from tankers direct to storage tanks on the shore, using buoyed pipelines. Shortly after, however, this means of delivery was replaced by a number of semi-permanent pipelines laid across the English Channel which were unwound from very large drums, towed by tugs. Terminal points were set up in Cherbourg, coming from the Isle of Wight and in Ambleteuse, with 16 pipelines coming from Dungeness. In both cases the fuel pipes were laid on the sea-bed and were given the acronym PLUTO (Pipe Line Under The Ocean). The back-up for this concept went far inland, and we later discovered that there was a relay pumping station just outside Bottesford, which sent tens of thousands of gallons of fuel across the Channel. It was all part of a quite incredible pre-arranged plan, which, when it came to the vital moment, worked absolutely to perfection and ensured the successful Invasion of Europe.

Much has been written about the process of pushing the German divisions further and further back, with the Battle of Normandy, the Falaise Gap, the Crossing of the Seine, followed by the Battles of the Ardennes, and the Crossing of the Rhine, with the Allied armies advancing into Germany from the west and south. At the same time, the Russians were smashing their way in from the east, which brought the European war to an end, with the two-pronged assault on Berlin.

All of this was achieved in just eleven months from the Normandy landings, but the Nazi war machine had by no means completely run down and there were still some unpleasant surprises in store for us. Exactly one week after D-Day, on 13th June 1944, the first four pilot-less 'flying bombs' crossed the British coast. Two days later, the Germans started in earnest their campaign of '*Vergeltung*' (Retaliation), when more than 200 bombs came over the Channel within twenty-four hours, culminating in 3,000 during the next five weeks. These bombs consisted of a pointed cylinder containing about a ton of high-explosive, fitted with short stubby wings and on top was mounted a small rocket motor. They were launched from inclined ramps in Holland and the Pas de Calais, roughly aimed towards London and the south-east, but once they were airborne had no guidance-system to direct them to any specific target. They were code-named 'V-1' by Hitler because he hoped they would be just the first of a series of terror weapons he planned to unleash against Britain. However, it was typical of Londoners that, having survived the Blitz, they treated these latest additions to the Nazi arsenal with complete contempt, nicknaming them 'Doodlebugs' or 'Buzz-bombs' – from the very uneven sound of their rocket engines. A great many never even got across the Channel, crashing into the sea, and relatively few reached London, falling-short in Kent – giving it the temporary sobriquet of 'Doodlebug Alley'.

Whenever one of these V-1s flew overhead, so long as one could hear the sound of its engine, one knew that it would continue to fly safely past. However, the moment the fuel was exhausted and the engine cut-out, the bomb would go into a silent glide, rapidly becoming a nose-dive, which ended with its detonation on hitting the ground, or some unfortunate building.

My only direct experience with a V-1 occurred when I was at Oakham. One night, just after we had gone up to bed, the sirens sounded. By that stage of the war, this was quite a rare occurrence because of our air-supremacy over Britain. Shortly afterwards we heard the unmistakable sound of a V-1 flying directly overhead and very foolishly crowded to the dormitory windows to see what was going on. A few minutes later we heard its engine cut-out and knew that it must have gone into its gliding nose-dive. Sure enough, a few seconds later we saw the flash as the bomb exploded on hitting the ground, but fortunately for us it was far enough away to avoid any of us being injured from flying glass. We were naturally very full of what we had seen, but when our House Master heard about it he was not in the least amused and we were given very strict instructions what precautions to take if it happened again, (which especially included NOT standing at windows).

During this time, London was still very much in the front line, as the V-1s continued to be a menace, and although they did not land in any one part of the city in any great numbers, they still constituted a threat. In fact, it seemed that so long as they landed somewhere on the mainland of Britain, and preferably in the London area, then that was sufficient to satisfy the Nazi warlords. By degrees, as the Allied armies over-ran the launching sites, the threat from these weapons diminished, but they still wrecked many buildings and caused loss of civilian life. During the bombardment about 750,000 houses were damaged, of which about 23,000 were totally destroyed, but in a strange sort of way they never seemed to constitute the danger of the conventional blitz in people's minds. The V-1s were intended to fly at a speed of about 400 mph, but very few ever managed to attain this, and consequently it was fairly simple to overtake them with a fighter and to shoot them down; but this was not quite as simple as it sounds, because the fighter-pilots had to fire from their maximum range to avoid being blown up when the bombs exploded in flight. Eventually, the V-1 bombardment ceased and we thought that the threat was over and done with.

We were wrong, however, because the Germans had a far more devastating weapon in their arsenal, which was a long-range rocket that they called V-2. After the war we learnt that these had been developed and tested at a secret research centre and rocket range, which had been built on the small island of Peenemünde, just off the German Baltic coast. These rockets were a very different concept when compared with their predecessors. They were fired vertically up into the air and reached a height of about 50 miles at the top of their trajectory.

They had a range of about 200 miles, but the single most significant difference was that they landed in an almost vertical nose-dive at a speed of about 4,000 miles per hour, their entire flight from launch site to target taking no more than three or four minutes. On 8th September 1944, just eight days after the V-1 attacks ceased, the Germans launched their first V-2s against London. Of course there was no warning whatsoever, nor could there be, and the first that we knew of these horrific weapons was a vast explosion – with no indication as to its cause. During the next seven months about 1,300 were fired at this country, but fortunately, like the V-1s before them, there were deficiencies in their guidance systems, which resulted in many falling short in the Channel. On average, they caused about twice the number of casualties as the earlier V weapons, but the extent of damage to buildings was greatly exceeded, as they carried about two tons of high explosive, and of course the sheer velocity at their point of impact greatly increased the overall detonation effect.

At that stage of the war, my sister Nancy had a job in London, working for the Chinese Free Press, and shared a flat with our brother Courtenay, who was at The Admiralty. One day she and a friend were shopping in Oxford Street during their lunch-break, and when they had finished, they queued for a bus to get them back to their office. When one eventually arrived, everybody tried to get on board, but the conductor protested that there were too many, and duly pushed off several of the would-be passengers, including my sister, telling them that there would be another bus along in a few minutes.

I may say that this was nothing particularly unusual in wartime London, but what followed shortly afterwards made this occasion horrifically different. The bus drove off down Oxford Street but when it was about half-a-mile away it suddenly disappeared in a massive explosion and cloud of flames and smoke, mixed with the dust from falling masonry from the buildings on either side. There was nothing left of the bus or its passengers and a great many passers-by were killed or injured as a result of this impact of yet another V-2.

As a direct result of this appalling experience Nancy returned to Bottesford for a much-needed rest and shortly after her arrival home was rushed off in an ambulance to Grantham Hospital. All this occurred just before I returned from Oakham for the school holidays, and on my arrival home I was told that Nancy had lost her baby. I remember being completely baffled at this news, because I had no idea that she even had a baby, and how on earth could she manage to lose it? It became clear to me that I still had a lot to learn about some of the 'facts of life', when it was explained that she had suffered a miscarriage. Nowadays it is hard to believe how children were kept in ignorance about such things at that time. Despite her dreadful experience, Nancy was up and about again very soon, and insisted on returning to London to carry on with her job, and although it may seem very 'British stiff upper-lip' in today's terms, I am quite certain that she felt that she just had to get over the trauma and to carry on, like so many other people placed in a similar position.

As the Allied armies swept the Germans further and further back, the launching of the V-weapons became increasingly spasmodic, and eventually ceased altogether. I have often thought, however, that if they had managed to make the aiming of these rockets more efficient so that they could have been used against the Normandy landings, history might have been very different.

A few months after her dreadful experience in Oxford Street, I was staying up in London with Nancy and Courtenay, when one evening they decided to ask some friends in for a meal. In the course of his travels, my brother had acquired a very handsome brass cannon, about nine inches long, which was a miniature replica of one the naval guns of Nelson's day. During the party, one of their guests was admiring the cannon, and in the ensuing conversation it transpired that it had never been fired, so it was decided that this should immediately be remedied.

In the course of some initial preparations a 12-bore shotgun cartridge was produced and carefully dissected, with the cordite removed and inserted in the muzzle of the cannon in the approved manner, using a pencil as a ramrod, and gently tamped down with bits of blotting-paper to serve as wadding. There was some discussion regarding a suitable location for the test-firing, but it was eventually decided that to aim it at the flat's fireplace would have to suffice. Everyone present took cover lying on the floor behind various pieces of furniture and my brother eventually lit the fuse. A few seconds later there was a flash and what sounded like a thunderous explosion and the room was full of smoke. When this had cleared, it was found that burning bits of wadding had ignited the unlit fire, which had been laid in the grate, which did not seem to matter very much, except that a few minutes later it became apparent that the chimney was on fire. For obvious reasons this was very much discouraged during wartime and a clear infringement of the Blackout Regulations, so my brother, accompanied by a couple of his guests, climbed through a skylight out onto the roof, where they located the burning chimney and promptly emptied a couple of fire-buckets of water down the flue. By the time they returned to the flat the fire had gone out, and although there was no water to be seen in the fireplace, they felt that they had fully achieved their objective.

It was not until next morning, when Courtenay was working in his office at The Admiralty, that his senior naval Commander came in, and during the course of their conversation, happened to remark that there must have been one hell of a storm during the night, because they had got up that morning to find floods of water had cascaded down into their fireplace. It was only at that moment that my brother remembered that the Commander had a flat in the same block, and needless to say, he made a few suitable comments about the vagaries of the weather but otherwise kept very quiet!

It became apparent that during the last stages of the war we had almost total air-supremacy; but even so, a few German fighter-bombers did sometimes make solo raids, and one night we were sitting in the drawing room at the Rectory, when we heard the sound of a low-flying aircraft, followed immediately by a burst of firing. Outside it was completely dark, and there had been no air-raid siren giving warning of an attack.

Flying operations had been taking place up at Normanton, and as usual the red lights on the top of the steeple were illuminated. Clearly (as we always feared) a German pilot had seen the lights and fired at them as he flew past, and as it was all over in a matter of seconds, there was really nothing to be done about it, except to check that all was well in the village. My father returned some time afterwards to tell us that everything was all right, and it was several weeks later that we learnt what had actually transpired, and in fact there were two sequels to this incident. First of all, we were told by a friend who worked in one of the Regional Control Rooms, that the aircraft in question had been part of a larger group that had been attacked when they crossed the Channel and had become separated from the rest. It would seem that the pilot had been trying to find his way back to base, but in this he was unsuccessful, as the plane was shot down by one of our own night fighter-pilots. The second point of interest was that a couple of days after the incident, when mowing the lawn, I came across two 20mm cannon shells which had been fired from the aircraft and had failed to explode on impact. I had them checked and the explosive removed, and still keep them as a special memento – because some months later we were told that this had actually been the very last raid against this country made by a piloted aircraft during the Second World War. This was not officially acknowledged until years afterwards, but finally it was announced that Bottesford had featured in the last air-raid.

7. Wartime Entertainment

During the Second World War entertainment was very much part of our lives, possibly far more so than in these present times, where we tend to take it all very much for granted. It is difficult to appreciate nowadays, with the vastly increased media coverage that we enjoy (or should I perhaps say 'endure'?), when every passing thought or whim can result in page after page of newspaper or magazine coverage, and hours on end of, very often, repetitive programmes on the television. At the beginning of the war, we had one wireless set which was contained in a fairly large wooden case, with a sunburst cut in the fretwood front. It got extremely hot due to the number of valves that it contained, and the tuning was very much a matter of hit or miss, and there was invariably a lot of background crackling noise. The programmes were fairly basic and the level of intellect was almost nil, but we thoroughly enjoyed what was available – albeit very little.

Perhaps because of these limitations, we tended to entertain ourselves far more than now, and everyone seemed to indulge in more conversation. As a family, we had always played games of one sort or another, because we actually enjoyed them. Certainly the Vicarage and the Rectory were always full of people that were either staying, or just calling in, and it was really quite unusual if nobody appeared round about eleven o'clock in the morning, for a cup of tea and a chat. Also, it was not in the least uncommon for someone to appear just before lunch, and inevitably they would be invited to share our meal. Possibly the reason for this was that my mother, being Irish, was extremely gregarious, and she loved to have people around her, and welcomed everyone with open arms. This was transmitted to the rest of us, and we just accepted the influx of people who appeared, including many that we knew, and several that we had never set eyes on before.

When she was working in the kitchen or out in the garden, my mother would frequently be singing quietly to herself, and although she was never what I would describe as musical, she certainly enjoyed many of the songs that everyone was singing at that time.

Looking back now, we did go in for some pretty asinine but very patriotic songs, like *Run Rabbit Run, We're Hanging out our Washing on the Siegfried Line, Kiss me Goodnight, Sergeant-Major* and *Roll out the Barrel*. There was one title that did not leave much to the imagination called *Roll Me Over, Lay Me Down and Do It Again*. Also some rather more nostalgic songs like: *There'll be Bluebirds over the White Cliffs of Dover*, and *A Nightingale Sang in Berkeley Square* and, when victory was in sight, a song called *I'm Going To Get Lit-Up When The Lights Go On in London*. But the most popular song of the war was the haunting German ballad *Lili Marlene*, originally written as a poem in 1915 by Hans Leip, who had been in love with two women called Lili and Marlene. He set it to music, but it was Norbert Schultze's melody that brought it to fame when it became widely known through a German singer, Lale Andersen, early in the war. In translation its sense was somewhat changed, but it was as popular with the British Army as it was with the Germans. In fact, at the end of the

North African Campaign in May 1943, when the 7th Armoured Division, on its way to the Allied victory parade in Tunis, passed the German 90th Light Division marching into captivity, both columns were singing the song.

There were a host of entertainers during the war of varying quality, but we all enjoyed listening to Gracie Fields, Vera Llynn, Flanagan & Allen, George Formby, Arthur Askey and so many more. Most of this entertainment came by way of the radio, and due to the wartime restrictions, it was some time before many of the theatres were able to renew their stage presentations. Some very attractive melodies came from these productions, such as the operettas of Ivor Novello, including *Glamorous Night* and *The Dancing Years*, which were both escapist romantic productions based upon an imaginary dream-land of 'Ruritania'. Another great British playwright was Noel Coward, who produced and acted in some excellent films of the war including *In Which We Serve* and *This Happy Breed*.

There were of course many others, but in particular two Americans provided the most astonishing break with tradition. In 1943, Richard Rodgers and Oscar Hammerstein presented a musical stage production called *Oklahoma!*, which swept us off our feet because it was such a tremendous contrast to anything we had seen before. Then, in the same year they produced another musical, *Carmen Jones*, which again, was completely different and a tremendous success. Since the Americans had arrived here in the war we had become accustomed to seeing coloured servicemen, but what was so extraordinary about that stage production, based upon Bizet's *Carmen*, was that the cast was entirely coloured.

I have already mentioned the dances in the Village Hall at Bottesford, but all over the country there was a large increase in the number of people attending dances of all sorts and descriptions. There were the big dance-halls like The Palais de Dance and even quite small restaurants that held *Thés Dansant* and all of these were immensely popular with the servicemen and women of every nationality. With the arrival of the Americans, we were introduced to a completely new form of dancing – with the Jitterbug, Swing, Jive and Be-bop and the songs of people like Perry Como, Bing Crosby, Frank Sinatra and so many more – all introduced by the Americans, but very quickly taken up by us too. They produced a new sort of sound in their 'big bands' with large numbers of instrumentalists, which led to the formation of a number of British bands that followed suite and very soon earned a great reputation for their excellent dance music.

The American servicemen had been largely responsible for the introduction of 'pin-ups' which appeared in many periodicals on our news-stands. Publications like *The New Yorker, Colliers, Harper's Bazaar* and *The Saturday Evening Post* were refreshingly different from anything that we had seen before, and the last of these had front covers often painted by a quite exceptional artist called Norman Rockwell. Several featured large fold-out centre pages of beautiful semi-nudes, which were quickly removed from their bindings, and pinned up on the walls of countless barrack-rooms, billets and even dug-outs during the course of the war. One of the best American artists to contribute to this demand was Alberto Vargas who produced some excellent paintings in *Esquire* which featured 'The Vargas Girls' – all of whom were beautiful and in various stages of undress. Copies of these paintings were commonly reproduced on the fuselages of aircraft and the sides of tanks and other fighting vehicles – to keep up morale.

One of the many British artists who featured during the war was Norman Pett, who produced daily cartoons which appeared in the *Daily Mirror* newspaper, which were extremely popular with the armed forces, and – I have to say – with schoolboys like myself. These daily contributions entitled 'Jane's Journal, the Diary of a Bright Young Thing' were all centred on a ravishing but slightly brainless blonde called Jane who appeared with her small dachshund (appropriately named 'Fritz').[1]

The one thing that appealed to Jane's male fans, (who must have been numbered in hundreds of thousands) was that in her various escapades she invariably seemed fated to become entangled with such mundane things as door handles, branches of trees and shrubs, in fact almost anything that might prove capable of causing her flimsy garments (both outer and under) to be torn or ripped off – leaving her in a state of total undress! Winston Churchill once jokingly dubbed her 'Britain's secret weapon' in homage to her role in raising and maintaining morale.

However, other cartoons that we saw during the war were used for far more serious purposes. Many appeared in

---

[1] illustration reproduced courtesy of Norman Pett / Mirror Newspaper Group.

newspapers, official pamphlets and on posters that were used to get over some particular point, and in one case even used in a training manual that was produced for soldiers serving in the jungles of the Far East.

One the earliest that I can recall was a cartoon by an artist who went under the name of Fougasse (the nom-de-plume of Kenneth Bird). It depicted two women chatting together while sitting in a bus, and seated directly behind them were Adolf Hitler and Hermann Göring and its very topical caption, intended as a stern reminder, was 'You never know who's listening. Careless Talk Costs Lives'. One of the other great cartoonists of the Second World War was an artist called David Low, and in the 8th June 1940 edition of the *Evening Standard* he showed an ancient paddle-steamer returning from Dunkirk, crammed with soldiers that had been rescued from the beaches, and in the background were a number of other little boats picking up the lines of soldiers who had waded out into the sea to meet them. It was very appropriately called 'To Fight another Day'. Ten days later he produced another patriotic cartoon depicting an English 'Tommy', standing on a clifftop facing the Channel, shaking his fist at a flight of Luftwaffe bombers flying towards him from the black clouds over Europe, with its apposite title, 'Very Well – Alone'.

The training manual produced for soldiers serving in the jungle, was illustrated by Fougasse, and I always remember a couple of pages which were intended to punch home an important message. One page showed a mass of jungle foliage with the very large rear view of an elephant, entitled 'What the soldier saw'. On the next page was a picture of a similar mass of jungle foliage, but nothing else – with the caption 'What the elephant saw'. The point being drummed home was that every soldier should be fully camouflaged while fighting in the jungle.

Here in Britain, we had become accustomed to the austerity of pretty dull-looking wartime publications, and even such excellent magazines as *Picture Post* mostly showed their pictures in black and white. With the advent of the American publications, however, everything was revealed – just like their films – "In Glorious Technicolor". Needless to say, we soon followed suit, and a number of very bright magazines were introduced like *Lilliput, Men Only* and *Readers' Digest* which were very popular small pocket-sized publications that provided a much needed measure of light relief, that contributed to the important feature of maintaining our high state of morale. No doubt today some would be considered very 'sexist', although I never recall hearing any women criticising them at the time, and just seemed to regard the pin-ups as good fun. It was, of course, a time of completely different standards created as an inevitable result of the war, but morality was probably far less lax than it is today, and in some ways we were considerably more restrained in what we read, heard or saw in the various forms of the media.

Also, there was a far greater sense of safety that existed in those days, when one considers that youngsters like myself did not hesitate to go off on a cycle-ride for several miles out into the countryside without fear of being accosted or waylaid. Equally, for those on foot, there was always the chance of 'thumbing a lift' which, again, was something introduced by the American servicemen. Anyone wanting a free ride, merely had to stand on the roadside and wave their thumb at any approaching vehicle, for the driver to stop and offer a lift. When I was at college, directly after the war, I often 'hitch-hiked' up to London, by this means, getting a ride from Bottesford into Grantham, and then walking out on The Great North Road, and easily getting a ride all the way (if the driver happened to be going in that direction), or perhaps using a number of separate lifts to cover the journey. In fact a far cry from the sort of conditions that exist today.

8. The Closing Stages of the War

In some ways, the closing stages of the Second World War seemed to pass very quickly, and although every single day had to be fought and won, we came eventually to that unforgettable moment when we heard of Adolf Hitler's suicide, along with his mistress Eva Braun, in the German High Command bunker beneath the burning and shattered streets that remained of Berlin. This sequence of events finally led up to the unconditional surrender of Nazi Germany to the Allies on 7th May 1945, whereby all hostilities ceased at midnight on the 8th May, which was declared to be V.E. Day – 'Victory in Europe Day'.

Of course the war in the Far East was to continue for a further three months, culminating in the Americans dropping an atomic bomb on Hiroshima on the 6th. of August, and another on Nagasaki three days later. This rapidly brought about the unconditional Japanese surrender on the 14th August 1945, and the following day was duly declared V.J. Day – 'Victory over Japan Day'. I suppose it is inevitable that V.E. Day made a larger impact upon most of us here in Britain, because of course the Germans had been a very real and tangible enemy whom we had often seen at first hand.

The Japanese war, on the other hand, was taking place on the other side of the world, and consequently far more remote. Nevertheless, for anyone like ourselves, who had members of the family fighting out in the Far East, it was just as real as the

European war. We could hardly believe it when the war was actually over, but to prove that it was, there were celebrations to mark both events held all over the country. I only witnessed those that took place on the 8th of May, when I was up in London staying with Nancy and Courtenay, and during breakfast heard the radio announcement that this was to be 'V.E. Day'.

We heard quite a lot of noise out in the street and realised that something very unusual was taking place, and on making some enquiries, we heard that crowds were converging on Buckingham Palace. We decided that we must go to join the masses of people who all seemed to feel a compelling need to share this unforgettable moment with the King and Queen who throughout the war, had constantly been the personification of our patriotism and loyalty. It may be something which is difficult for later generations to ever appreciate or understand, but we all felt that, as Winston Churchill remarked, this was our 'Finest Hour'. All the hardships and deprivations that we had endured for so long, were made worthwhile by the feeling of fellowship and sharing in which we had all so willingly taken part.

There can be no doubt that the King and Queen were much loved, and for anyone like ourselves who made their way to the front of Buckingham Palace on that memorable day, the sheer outburst of excitement can never be fully described. We found ourselves amongst literally thousands of people, and to this day I will never quite understand how we managed to get within ten feet of the Palace railings. The gates were firmly shut, and in addition to the usual palace guard, there were a number of policemen on duty, but of course they were completely swallowed up in the vast crowd which was simply bursting with pent-up emotion.

There was almost continuous laughter, singing, dancing and cheering, and so long as I live, I will never again experience such concentrated high spirits and good humour that we witnessed and in which we took part, on that memorable day. The crowd was made up of thousands of men and women in uniform from all the services, and included every conceivable nationality. There were also a great many civilians, many of whom had taken their children along with them to share in an experience that they would never forget for the rest of their lives.

Somehow, out of all that marvellous myriad of celebration, one small but amusing incident comes to mind. At one stage, our attention was drawn to an American sailor who had managed to climb right up to the top of one of the gate pillars of the Palace, which must have been about twenty feet high, and to judge from his antics, and the way in which he was swaying about while clinging to the lantern on top of the pillar, he was already in high spirits – in more ways than one. Clearly there was a distinct risk of him falling and seriously injuring himself, quite apart from those that he might land upon; and to everyone's delight, a London Bobby proceeded to climb up the pillar after him, with cheers of encouragement spurring him upwards every inch of the way. When he eventually reached the top, the American sailor flung his arms around him in a welcoming embrace, and the Bobby responded magnificently by suggesting that the two of them should exchange hats. Somehow or other, he managed to persuade the sailor to return to the safer level of the pavement, and the two them descended without mishap, to more cheers and laughter.

All of this reached its climax of course, when the King and Queen, accompanied by the two Princesses, appeared on the balcony directly in front of us, and between them – at the King's insistence, was the Prime Minister, Winston Churchill.

If the cheers had been loud before, they then became absolutely deafening, as the vast throng of people were quite overcome by the emotions prompted by this truly historic occasion.

During the three months which followed V.E. Day, there was a certain sense of anti-climax for many people, and all that they could think about was the return home of all the tens of thousands of servicemen and women. However, for many like ourselves, who still had relatives fighting in the Far East, the war was by no means over.

To remind us of this, although none was needed, the lists of casualties published daily, continued to show the toll in human life. The Americans had managed to turn the tide completely against the Japanese in the Pacific, and very gradually, island by island, they were pushed back towards their starting point in Japan. There is no doubt at all that this was proving to be a slow and very costly process in terms of loss of human life, and it is not really surprising therefore that the Americans decided to speed things up in the most dramatic and devastating way.

The dropping of the Atomic Bombs on Hiroshima and Nagasaki inevitably shocked the whole world, and there have been recriminations and heart-searching by some people ever since. However, there was always the counter-argument that the dropping of those two bombs undoubtedly saved thousands of Allied lives, which would otherwise have been lost, and without question it certainly produced the desired effect in the speedy unconditional surrender of Japan.

My eldest brother Rodney, was one of those that did not return home until some months after V.J. Day, as he was still out in Burma, where he had taken part in what proved to be the longest land campaign of the war, fighting against the Japanese in the action on the River Irrawaddy, and around Imphal From the outbreak of war he had enlisted in the Royal Artillery, and joined the 115th Field Regiment which was formed in Leicester, under the command of a Colonel Simpson. Like all Gunners, Rodney spent time at Larkhill, and was commissioned shortly afterwards. Having been posted to the East Coast, just after Dunkirk, the regiment was sent out to India to join S.E.A.C. (South East Asia Command). Following a period of training in Ceylon and then at Bangalore in India, they were moved into Burma, as part of the 19th Indian ('Dagger') Division, under the command of General (later Field Marshal) Slim.

For a great deal of his time in Burma, Rodney acted as F.O.O. (Forward Observation Officer), and this entailed moving as far forward as possible, in order to see, and to report back, where the shells were falling. In this he was given the protection of a detachment of Ghurkas, with whom he got on extremely well, and I find it not in the least surprising that they earned his very highest respect, as some of the finest infantry soldiers in the world. When he left them to return home, their Subahdar presented him with a very fine Kukri, which had been made for him by one of the Ghurkas – who particularly liked to use the steel from the springs of abandoned Bedford army lorries.

When he eventually returned home he was a very changed person, having lost a lot of weight and looking quite gaunt. At that time, Rodney, Courtenay and I shared one large bedroom at Bottesford Rectory, which was always known as 'The Boys' Room', and on arrival his luggage was placed on the floor; and I can recall the rather musty smell of Teak and Sandalwood which he had brought with him, straight from the Burmese jungle. The first evening after his return I went up to bed before the others, and was lying down reading a book with my dog asleep on my feet. Suddenly, he sat bolt upright and stared at the floor beyond the end of the bed, and the hackles rose up on his back. Getting up to see what had frightened him, I saw a dark red tarantula spider which must have been about eight inches across, slowly crawling over the carpet – obviously feeling the change of climate. Picking up the small coal-scuttle from the fireplace, and popping it straight over it, I then slid a magazine under, and with the spider securely trapped, took it down the back stairs and out into the yard where it was speedily despatched. Rodney was rather perturbed by this, and searched through the rest of his luggage very carefully, and we were all relieved that no more jungle specimens were found, but I have to admit that thereafter, I was never very fond of spiders – especially large ones.

His luggage however, did reveal some other reminders of living in those conditions, because we noticed that the leather of his boots had completely rotted away, along with some of his webbing equipment. Almost anything made of paper, like letters, magazines, etc., had disintegrated due to the intense humidity.

A day or so after his return home, my brother made a name for himself as a lighter of fires. For some unexplained reason, the fireplace in the Drawing Room at the Rectory had always been difficult to light, which may have been due to lack of draught, as all the windows were sealed due to my efforts with cotton-wool. Every fire that we tried to light seemed to go out after a few minutes, and it often took a number of attempts before we succeeded. I was commenting on this when Rodney happened to overhear me, and straightway he offered to show me how it should be done, using the technique that he had adopted in the jungle, even with wood that was soaking wet. A brief trip out into the garden produced some twigs and branches and a handful of moss, which he carefully laid in the grate building up a small cone. He then twisted a newspaper into a very tight spiral, which he placed in a cavity that he had left underneath.

The great moment for lighting at last arrived, and we all stood around to watch the demonstration, and only my father was absent as he was over in the church. My brother put a match to the paper spiral, and after a few minutes we had quite an impressive blaze beginning to burn. Unfortunately, the Drawing Room fireplace must have been somewhat more restricted than the open expanses of the Burmese jungle, because in a very short time it became quite obvious that the chimney was on fire – something of which my brothers seem to make a habit. We raked out the burning debris from the fireplace and some of us went outside to see flames emerging from the chimney-pot, with clouds of smoke which billowed around us.

At that moment my father returned, and glancing up, he remarked that he was glad to see that I had at last managed to get the fire to light.

We put out the fire in the chimney by stuffing a wet sack up the flue, and this very quickly did the trick, but we were left with rather a mess in the fireplace which took some time to clear up.

As I write this, in a few days time it will be Armistice Sunday, and of course that is a good time for remembering. Mention of the fact has already been made, that my father was a Chaplain to the Forces in the Great War, serving in Northern Italy on the River Piave campaign. When it came to the Second World War, he was appointed as an Honorary Chaplain to the Forces, and this chiefly applied during the earlier years, when we were still in Leicester.

During the war, and afterwards, at every Remembrance Service each Armistice Sunday, there were almost always parades which included, first and foremost, any active service units that were available to parade, and many took part bringing with them their flags or standards. These invariably included members of The British Legion, who so proudly carried their Legion Standards on such occasions, and sometimes in addition, there would be flags paraded by the Boy Scouts, the Girl Guides and any other organizations that had them. There was one thing that my father had done on his arrival in the village, which had received general approval. He had noticed that there was no means of flying a flag on the church, because unlike so many that had towers, the spire would have been in the way and made it quite impossible to erect a pole. However he got round this problem by having a tall flagpole erected just beside the South Porch, which was the main means of access into the church, and from that moment on, The Union Flag or The Cross of St. George were flown on regular occasions.

The Remembrance Services were always deeply moving, and I can always think back to the quiet metallic clink of medals, proudly worn by anyone entitled to do so. Naturally, this included my father, who always displayed his medal-ribbons on his Chaplain's stole, and the actual medals each Armistice Sunday. He was never a pacifist, and I have no doubt that his success and popularity, particularly with the men in his parishes, was entirely due to the fact that he made himself one of them, unlike some clergy, who seem determined to set themselves apart.

On the first Armistice Sunday that the Americans were up at Normanton, my father invited the Commandant to take part in the Remembrance Service, and this was enthusiastically accepted. About a hundred of them arrived before the service, carrying no less than three flags, and they even produced an extra one which my father had hoisted up on the flagpole, and there we saw the wonderful sight of The Union Flag and the American 'Old Glory' flying side by side. They also brought a trumpeter who played the Last Post with quite a swing. At the beginning of the service, the standard-bearers slow-marched up the Aisle to my father, who received them on the steps of the Sanctuary, directly in front of the Altar. There he carried-out one particular bit of ceremonial that I had never seen performed by any other clergyman. I can only think that it was something peculiar to Army padres, but whatever the reason, it was certainly impressive.

At such services, it was the normal practice for most clergy to merely receive the flags, and then to stand them in each corner of the Sanctuary on either side of the Altar; but my father's technique was quite different. On receiving each flag, he would immediately turn, facing towards the Altar, allowing the flag to fly loosely from its pole, and with a distinct flourish, he would then lay the pole lengthwise across the Altar, so that the flag or standard draped down across the frontal, clearly displayed.

It is funny how different things appeal to different people, because I can remember after that service, the American Commandant and a number of the servicemen commented on the way in which this had been done, saying how greatly they admired it. I don't think that any of them had seen it before, and it obviously made quite an impression which was appreciated, because thereafter, my father always had the most wonderful relationship with all of the British Legion – of which he had been a member ever since The Great War.

At all those Remembrance Services each Armistice Sunday, we always heard (and have continued to do so, year after year) those four epic lines written by Lawrence Binyon, which state :

"They shall grow not old, as we that are left grow old:
Age shall not weary them, nor the years condemn.
At the going down of the sun and in the morning
We will remember them."

I don't suppose when he first wrote those lines, that Binyon could possible have imagined the countless thousands of times that they would be repeated, all over the world. Somewhat less known is the fact that they were set to music in 1915 by Sir

Edward Elgar, under the title 'For the Fallen', which formed a part of his suite 'The Spirit of England', Op.80, written for Soprano, Tenor, Chorus and Orchestra. Those four lines of verse seem to encapsulate the feelings of us all, and to reiterate our promise – that, come what may, – we will remember those that died.

Thinking back to those services, I am reminded most vividly of one quite extraordinary occasion, which took place at Bottesford. Since they were first conceived in 1867, a series of conferences have been held in London, every ten years or so, for all of the Bishops of the Anglican Communion.

As customary, these take place at Lambeth Palace, and consequently are known as The Lambeth Conferences. In a gesture of world-wide reconciliation after the war, Doctor Fisher, who was Archbishop of Canterbury at the time, arranged for one of these meetings to be held in 1948. As usual, immediately afterwards many of the Bishops accepted invitations to go and preach to congregations all over the country, but as may be imagined there were never enough to go round. My father decided to apply, as he had met the Archbishop on several occasions in the past, when my eldest brother Rodney was Head Boy of Repton during Doctor Fisher's Headmastership. He was particularly pleased when he received a reply from the chaplain to the Bishop of Assam, accepting his invitation for the Bishop to come and preach at Bottesford. By this time my father had been appointed Rural Dean of the Framland I Deanery, which included several local parishes, and there was little doubt that the opportunity of hearing one of the 'Lambeth Bishops' actually preaching to us, was considered something of a coup, not only in Bottesford, but in the whole area.

On the day the weather was simply atrocious as it was wet, windy and very cold. Having driven from London, the Bishop and his chaplain were due to arrive at the Rectory in time for tea, as he was due to preach at Evensong. Just before three o'clock the car arrived at the front door and out got the chaplain and it was immediately apparent that he was a very worried man. He helped the Bishop out of the car, and we instantly realised that he was a native of Assam and appeared to be unwell. He was literally shaking with the cold and very feeble and unsteady on his feet, and had to cling on to his chaplain's arm as they came into the house. When my father and mother were introduced to him he just smiled and nodded, but it seemed that he could scarcely understand what was being said. When he had taken off his coat, the four of them went into the Study, where he virtually collapsed on the sofa in front of the fire.

He was plied with cups of hot tea in an effort to warm him up, but his chaplain was clearly very concerned and distressed, as it seemed extremely unlikely that the Bishop would be able to take part in the special service. My mother suggested calling the doctor, but this the Bishop completely rejected and just asked if he might rest for a while. The feelings of my father and mother can perhaps be imagined, because so much preparation had gone into this visit, with a large congregation expected, and it seemed that the whole thing was turning into a complete fiasco.

The chaplain said that he would like to stay with the Bishop while he rested, and my father came through to join the rest of us in the Drawing Room. Naturally he was looking very worried, not only regarding the Bishop, but also because it seemed distinctly possible that the whole service might have to be cancelled, with no way of informing anyone who might want to attend – until they actually arrived at the church.

When it came to the time to get ready for the service, we found that the Bishop was looking somewhat better, although he was obviously still feeling the ill-effects of our climate. He made it clear to his chaplain that he had every intention of attending the service, and was duly helped to change into his robes. Completely unaware of all this drama, the two Churchwardens arrived with their wands of office to escort the Bishop over to the church; and with some of us trying to hold umbrellas over them against the driving rain, we slowly made our way through the garden, over the bridge and into the church. The service started and the choir and clergy processed slowly up the Aisle, and many of the congregation turned to take their first surreptitious look at a coloured Bishop. Apart from knowing that he came from Assam which was part of India, I don't think any of us knew much more about him, and of course the congregation had no means of knowing that he had arrived in such a state of ill-health.

My father led him up to his stall in the Sanctuary where he sat alone, a small hunched-up figure who remained seated for the greater part of the service that followed. The rest of us carried on in the usual way, singing the canticles, psalm and hymns. The church was absolutely packed, with extra seats placed in the side-aisles to accommodate one of the largest congregations that anyone could recall. There were a great many children with their parents, and inevitably this produced the sort of fidgeting and background noises associated with children in church. When it came to the moment in the service for the Bishop to deliver his sermon, my father escorted him to the pulpit, allowing a good deal more time than usual for this. He then watched with some trepidation as the Bishop very slowly climbed up the pulpit steps, gripping tightly on to the carved banister rail. We continued singing the last few lines of the hymn and all eyes were concentrated on the bowed figure standing in the pulpit.

At the end of the hymn, we waited as customary for a few words by way of preface before we were seated. Instead there was complete silence, and after a moment or two with nothing happening, we all sat down. You could have heard the proverbial pin drop and we all watched as the most amazing transformation took place before our eyes. The Bishop slowly straightened up and turned to look around at all of us sitting in the body of the church, and smiling at us he then began to speak. He continued to preach to us for over thirty minutes, in a voice that seemed to gather strength as he spoke, and during the whole of that long sermon there was not another sound to be heard. The children just sat spell-bound as we listened to every word, and despite his accent we fully understood everything that he said. In fact, the change in his voice was so dramatic, having been almost unable to communicate when he first arrived, that we began to wonder if we had all been mistaken, but after his sermon he returned to his stall, obviously exhausted.

After the service we returned to the Rectory, and shortly afterwards the Bishop and his chaplain left to go back to London. Although my mother tried to persuade him to stay the night and return next day, he declined this offer with grateful thanks and explained that there was another church in north London, where he was due to preach next morning.

There is a sad sequel to this story, because we heard later that following his return to Assam, the Bishop died shortly afterwards, and I know that my father and mother were convinced that it was due to our climate. For those of us who were present at that service in Bottesford church, nothing could make us forget the quite extraordinary experience of hearing a man, who could hardly speak any English, addressing a congregation for so long, and to be wholly understood.

Of course, as Christians we are brought up to believe in the gift of The Holy Spirit, and for some time after that memorable service my father was rather quiet and thoughtful; but I have no doubt whatsoever that he felt, as I think we all did, that that was exactly what we had witnessed on that unforgettable occasion. The rest of the congregation never knew what had occurred, but at least the two Churchwardens sensed that something strange had been going on, and were deeply impressed when my father told them all about it afterwards.

EPILOGUE

I think that it may be appropriate to conclude by mentioning what was really the final chapter of the Second World War, so far as my life in Bottesford was concerned. During the last years of the fighting it was decided to set up a War Memorial Committee, to consider some form of tangible reminder of the war and to commemorate the names of those from the village who had died during the conflict.

The intention was to erect a memorial plaque in the church, and if sufficient funds were received, to build a new village hall to replace the old corrugated-iron structure that had been there since The Great War. As it turned out, The War Memorial Fund raised a substantial sum, and clearly far more than would be needed for the plaque, and it was realised that there would be enough to afford the new building which was to be called The Memorial Hall.

All of the necessary consents were obtained, and a local builder's quotation was accepted and the work was put in hand. It was duly completed on time, and thereafter the villagers enjoyed all of the advantages of an up-to-date building which was properly insulated, heated and lit. It was provided with its own kitchen and servery, also suitable lavatory accommodation and rooms for meetings, storage, etc..

In 1948 the Committee met again in order to discuss the Memorial Plaque for the church, and I was extremely touched when they invited me to design this for them, especially as I was not yet qualified, and only in the third, of a seven-year architectural course. Although this was pointed out at the time, the committee were adamant that I should carry out the work, and naturally I was delighted to do so. In fact I still have the original Sketch Design that is dated 29th November 1948, which illustrated the preliminary design proposals.

In Bottesford Church, the memorial plaque for The Great War was an unusually fine example, with a large, single limestone slab on which were engraved the names of all those who had died; with their regimental badges, cast in bronze, and set into the stone alongside each name. The stone slab was set within a beautifully carved decorative alabaster frame. I proposed that the new plaque should employ the same two materials of limestone and alabaster.

Also, that bronze badges should again be included, and made by the same firm, The Dryad Metal Company of Leicester, that made those on the first memorial. As there was scarcely enough space to fit the new plaque on the wall beneath the original memorial, I suggested removing two pews and a portion of the timber floor on which they stood, along with the length of dado that formed the inside ends of the pews against the wall. This would provide sufficient wall space to enable the new plaque to be positioned directly beneath the original, so that the two were closely related together. In addition, I suggested that stone paving should be laid instead of the timber flooring, so that a recess was formed off the South Aisle, with a stone shelf across the inside face, on which flowers or wreaths could be placed. Finally, it was proposed that two bronze brackets should be mounted, one on each side of the combined memorial, to carry the British Legion Standard and the Union Flag – the latter having been donated to the church by a Major Wright, who had served in the Far East and had been a prisoner of the Japanese throughout the greater part of the war.

All of these proposals were embodied in another sketch dated 3rd July 1949 and the whole design was accepted by the Committee and the work put in hand. Then on 31st October 1950, five years after the end of the war, a special service was held in Bottesford Church when the new War Memorial was dedicated by the Bishop of Leicester.

In his address, he was kind enough to remark on the fact that the committee had invited me to design the memorial, as he felt that it was an especially good example of using the talents available within our own community. The main subject of his address was based upon the five notes of : Remembrance, Reverence, Re-affirmation, Resolution and Recollection. This service of dedication and especially the Bishop's words struck a chord which will long vibrate in the minds of all who were present.

Like many other families, we survived the war, but as was so often the case, with our own losses. My brother Rodney almost lost the sight of his eyes due to some bug that he picked up in the jungle, and of course my sister Nancy lost her baby as a result of her narrow escape from a V2. Her husband Robert, was much affected by all of his experiences in North Africa and Italy, and although he was Mentioned in Despatches, he would never talk about or discuss any action in which he had taken part during the war. My cousin George Young was killed in action in Normandy soon after D-Day, and his sister Beatrice lost her husband, who, as a bomber pilot, was shot down over

Hamburg. Several of the boys with whom I had been at school were killed, and in Leicester and at Bottesford there were men and women that we knew from both parishes, who died.

Sometimes one hears people ask if the war was ever necessary, what it achieved and if it was all worthwhile.

To any of those sort of questions there can only be one answer – unless one happens to be so selfish and hidebound as to ignore the reason for entering the war in September 1939 – which was, quite simply, to survive as a nation.

It should never be forgotten that by the time that it was all over, we had seen the German conquest of most of Europe, and in the Far East we had witnessed the seemingly unstoppable rise and expansion of the Japanese Empire, with its occupation of most of the Pacific islands, with the very real threat of the invasion of Australia and New Zealand. We had seen the persecution and near-genocide of the Jews, and the unspeakable cruelty shown to military prisoners of war and civilians alike, in the horrific Nazi concentration Camps at such places as Belsen, Büchenwald and Dachaü and the Japanese internment camps in Malaya and Burma. Such niceties as the rules laid down in The Geneva Convention were often ignored in what had been a world-wide conflict.

We were faced with destruction of civilization, as we knew it, by two nations on opposite sides of the globe, who seemed dead set on achieving 'world domination'. That we should have beaten both of them in the span of six years was something of which we could justifiably be proud, but the cost in terms of loss of human life was immeasurable.

If viewed dispassionately, and for anyone of my generation it is completely unthinkable that there should be any attempt to suppress the facts, or perhaps to try and pretend that it never took place. To me it seems appalling that nowadays our system of state education is unwilling to recall these events, and in many schools we find that History is no longer even part of the syllabus. It seems incredible that children should be debarred from knowing, and understanding, the reason why so many of their grandparents died in the war, and the sacrifices that were made. It is of course inevitable that the numbers attending the annual Armistice Sunday services and memorial celebrations each year become less and less, which is the natural sequence of events as the older generations die off. However, it is important that the young should continue to celebrate what for them, is the reason for their very existence, and with that vital understanding, to be thankful in their own small way, and perhaps most important of all – to never forget.

The Bottesford War Memorial, sketched by the author in 1949

POSTSCRIPT

The writing of these memories of The Second World War was completed just before Christmas in 2002.

At this time, the Vicarage of St. James the Greater in Leicester, remains very much the same as I remember it, and is still the house provided for the incumbent.

At Bottesford, however, a new Rectory has been built on another site in the village, and the old building and the land on which it stands, has been converted to provide nineteen dwellings, called Rectory Court, comprising four houses, four bungalows and eleven apartments.

SIC TRANSIT GLORIA MUNDI.

BIBLIOGRAPHY

The Second World War by Winston S. Churchill, Cassell & Co Ltd, 1954.

The Oxford Companion to the Second World War, edited by
I.C.B. Dear, Oxford University Press, 1995.

Were Those the Days? by Stanley Blackmore, Saracen Publications, 1997.

My Memoirs by Alfred T.G. Blackmore, Edited by A.S.G. Blackmore, Saracen Publications, 2000.

The Times Atlas of The Second World War, edited by John Keegan, Times Books Ltd, 1989.

The London Road, Leicester with St James the Greater church and vicarage. From a watercolour by S. W. A. Newton, 1924.
(reproduced courtesy of Dr. A.D. McWhirr, FSA).

Author's impression of the evacuation at Dunkirk, 1940, from a sketch made at the time.

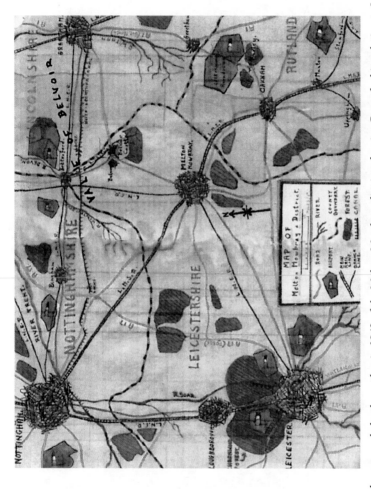

A sketch map made by the author in 1943 of the Melton Mowbray district, showing Bottesford in relation to Leicester.

Bottesford Rectory, St Mary's Church and part of the centre of the village, including the Red Lion Inn. (Ken Greasley Ltd)

Fleming's bridge across the River Devon near Bottesford Rectory.
This ancient packhorse bridge dates from c.1600. (Ken Greasley Ltd)

Belvoir Castle (photo taken by my late Father)

The east side of Bottesford Rectory from the garden. (Ken Greasley Ltd)

The garden of Bottesford Rectory and St Mary's Church, showing the side lawn, with its backdrop of trees, including an ancient cedar of Lebanon, a large copper beech, a lime and a Spanish chestnut. (Ken Greasley Ltd)

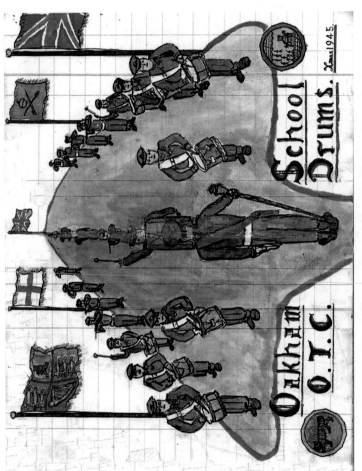

Oakham School OTC Drums in 1945, as depicted by the author at the time.

D- Day 1944 as recorded by the author at the time.

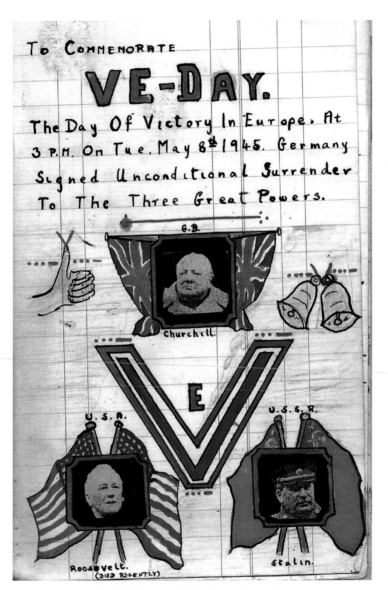

VE Day 1945 as recorded by the author at the time.

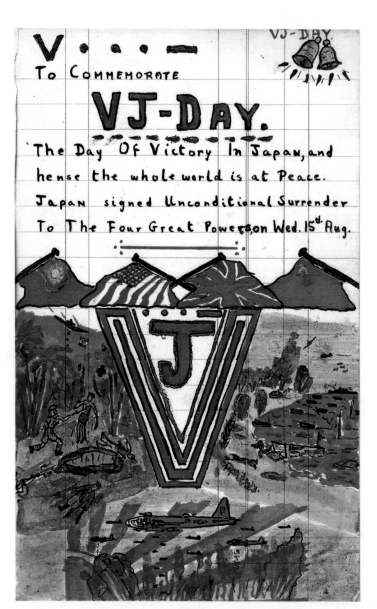

VJ Day 1945 – as recorded by the author at the time.

British War Medal 1914-18   Victory Medal   Defence Medal.   War Medal 1939-45
(with Mentioned in Dispatches clasp)

My father's medals from both world wars.